EASTER MANDALA

ADULT COLORING BOOK

This Book Belongs To

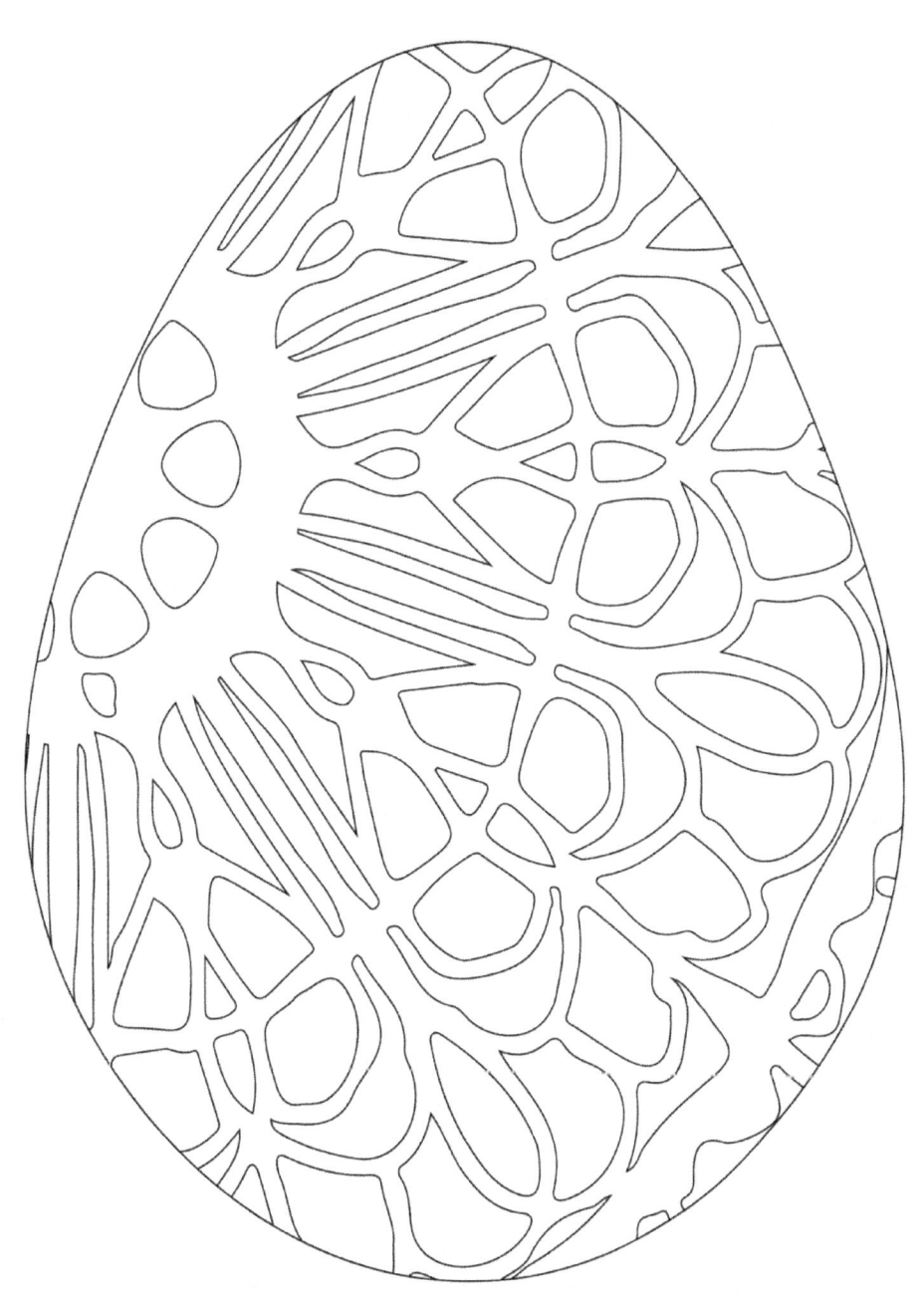

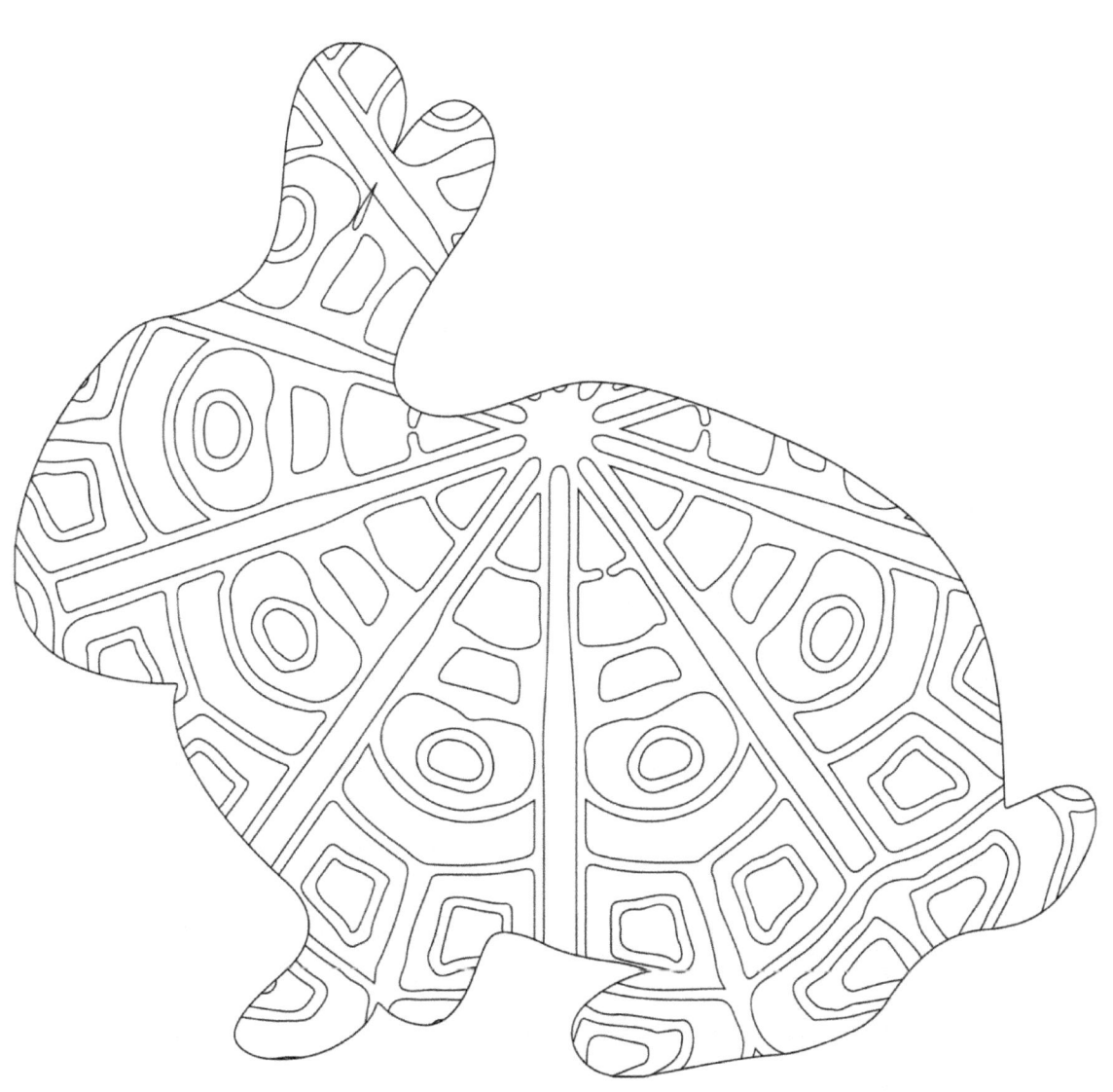

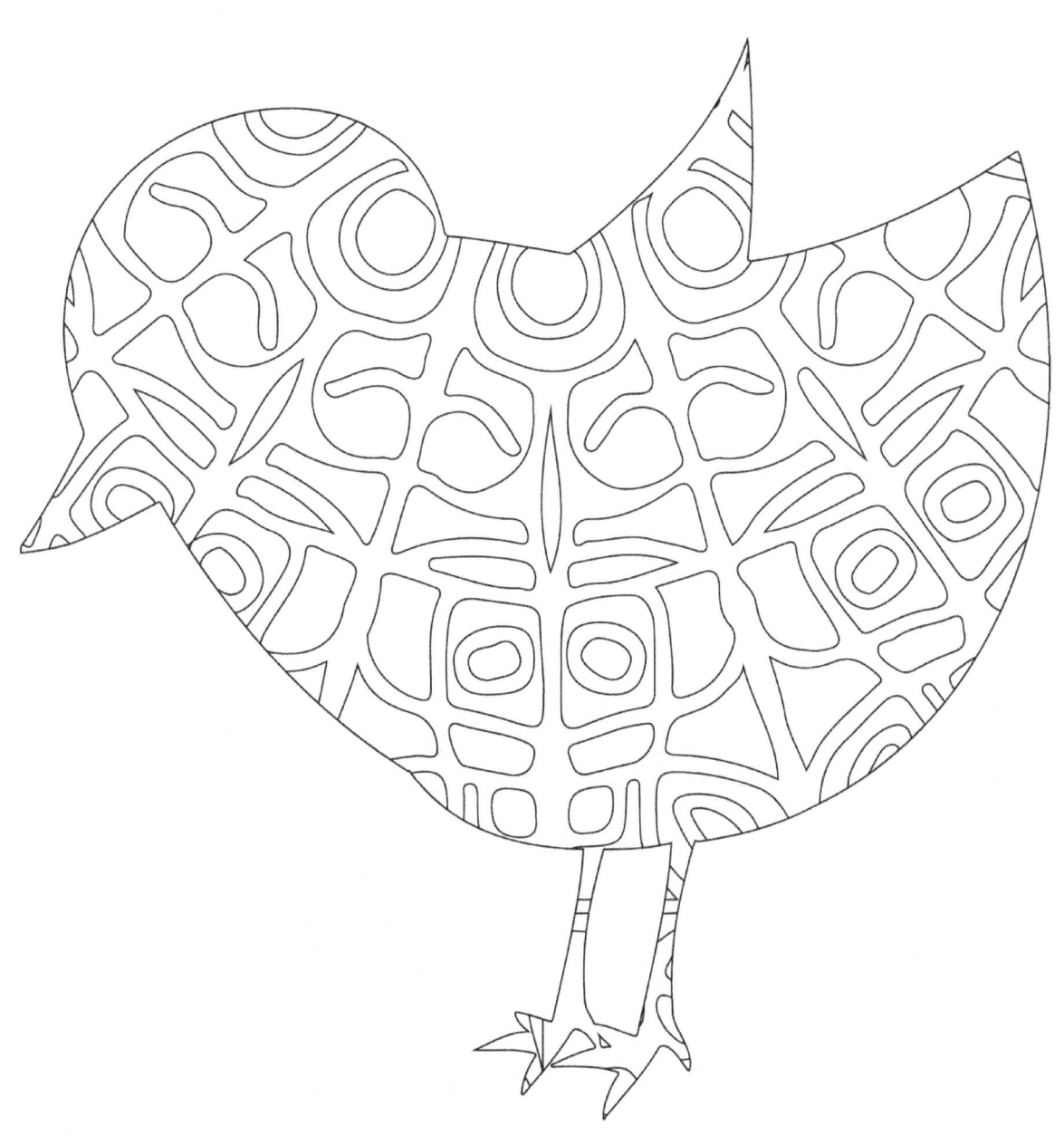

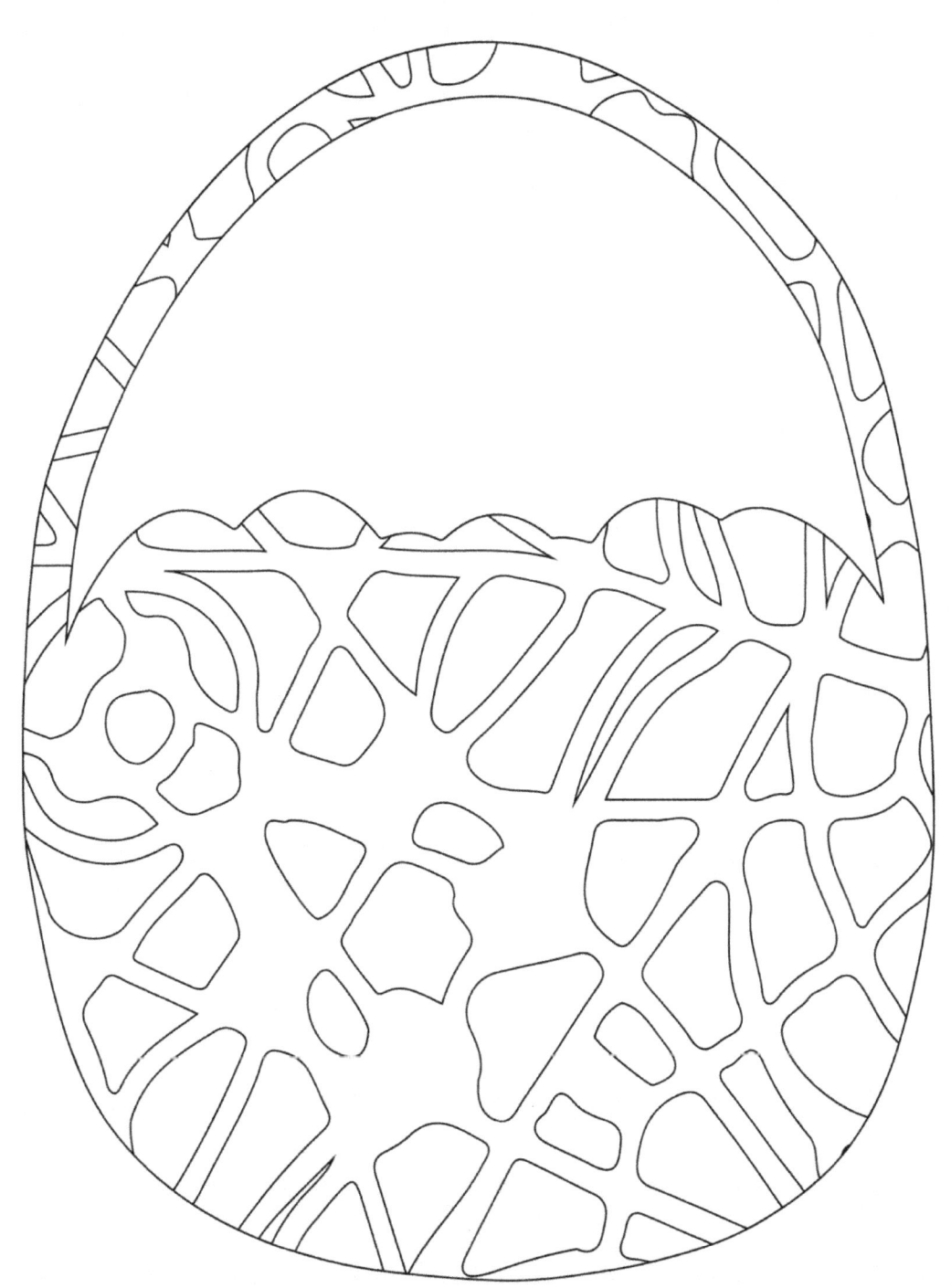

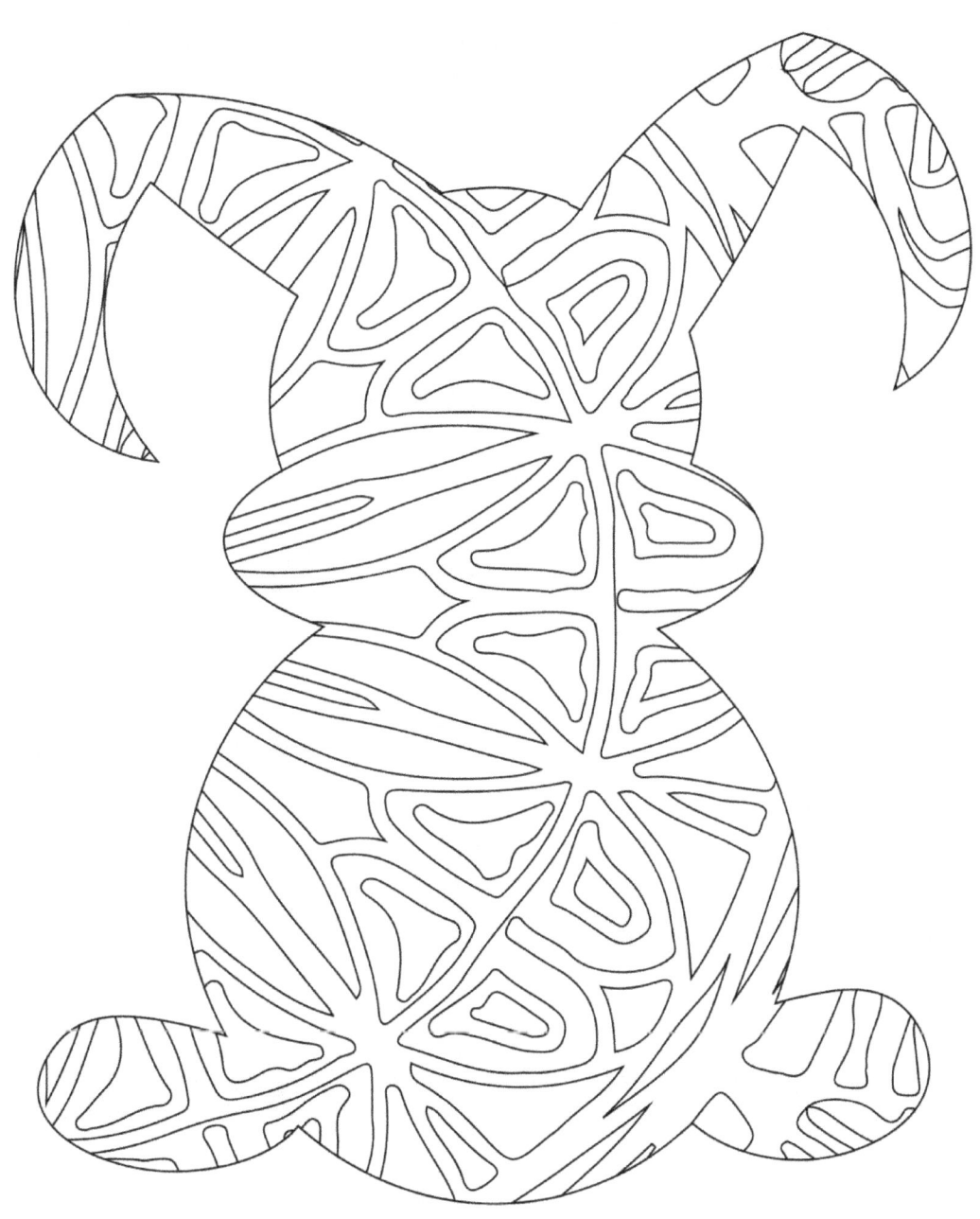

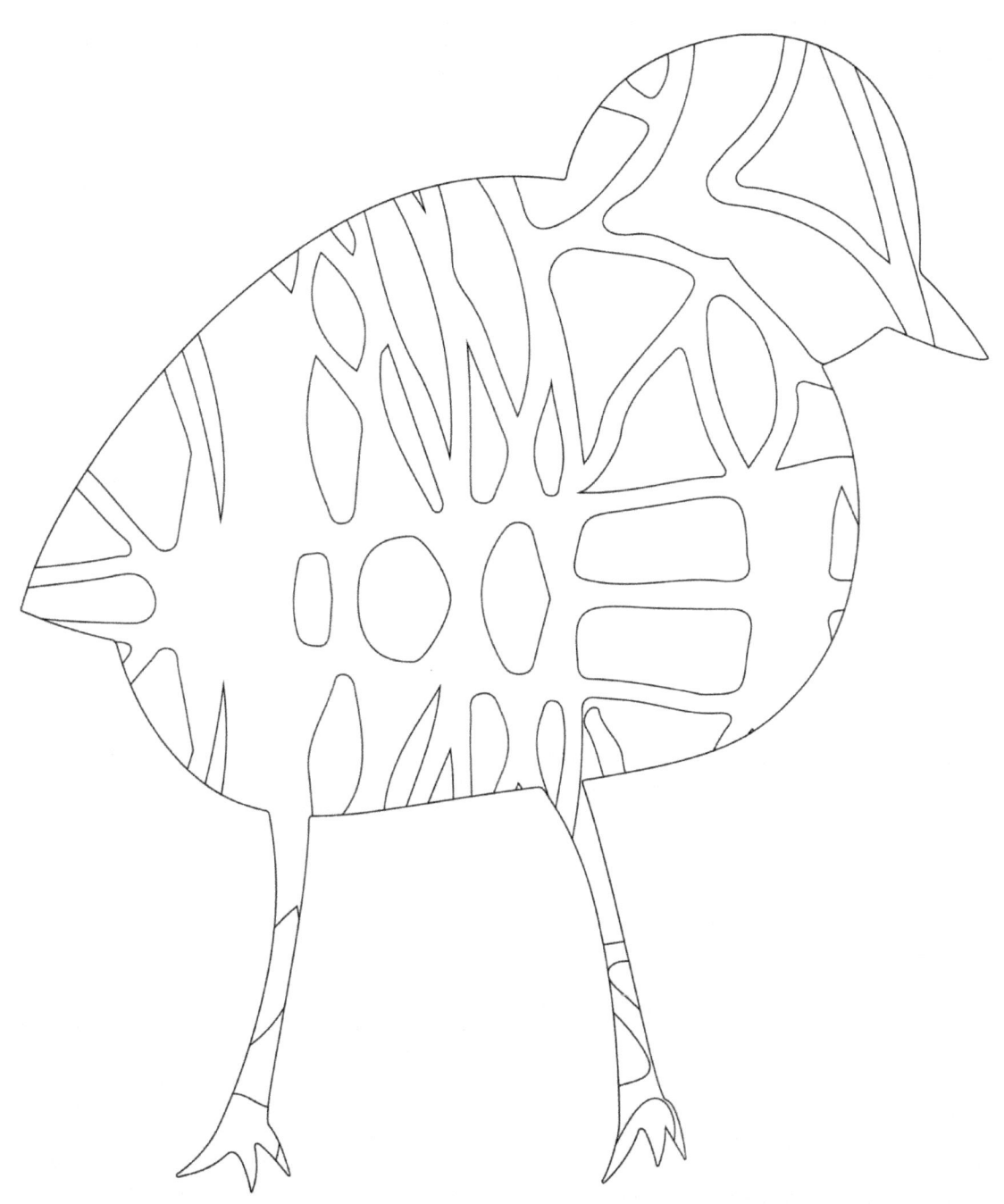

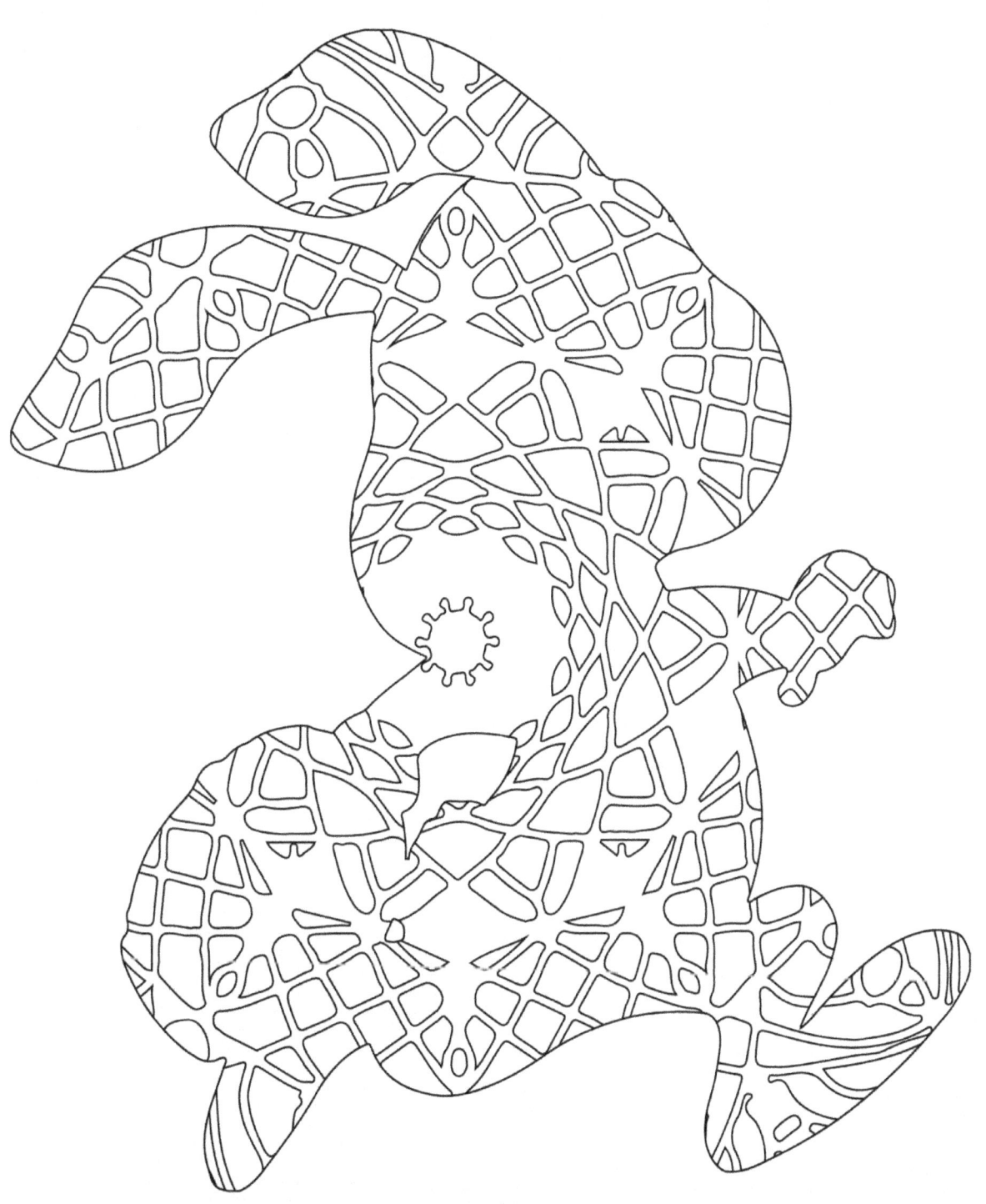

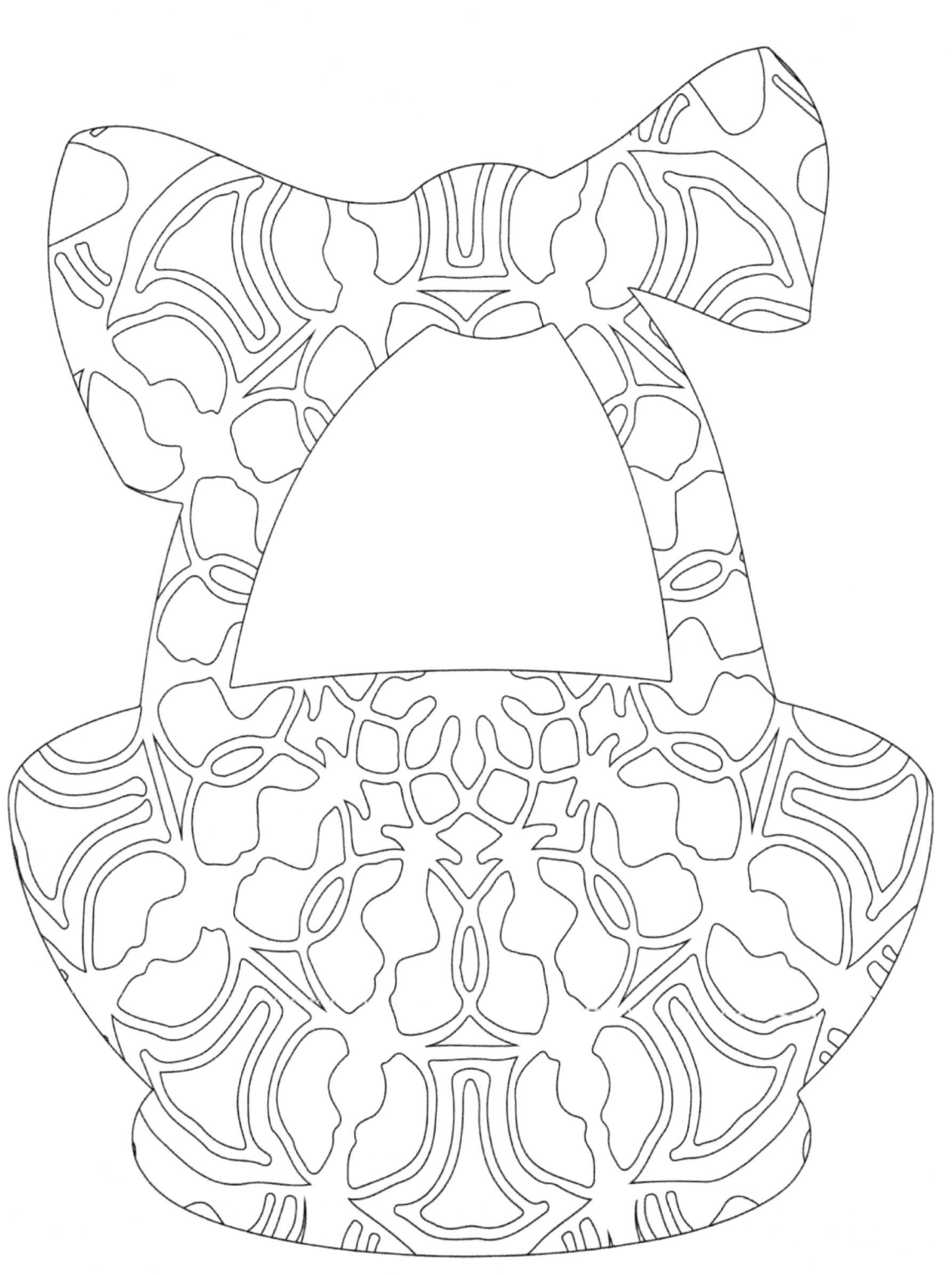

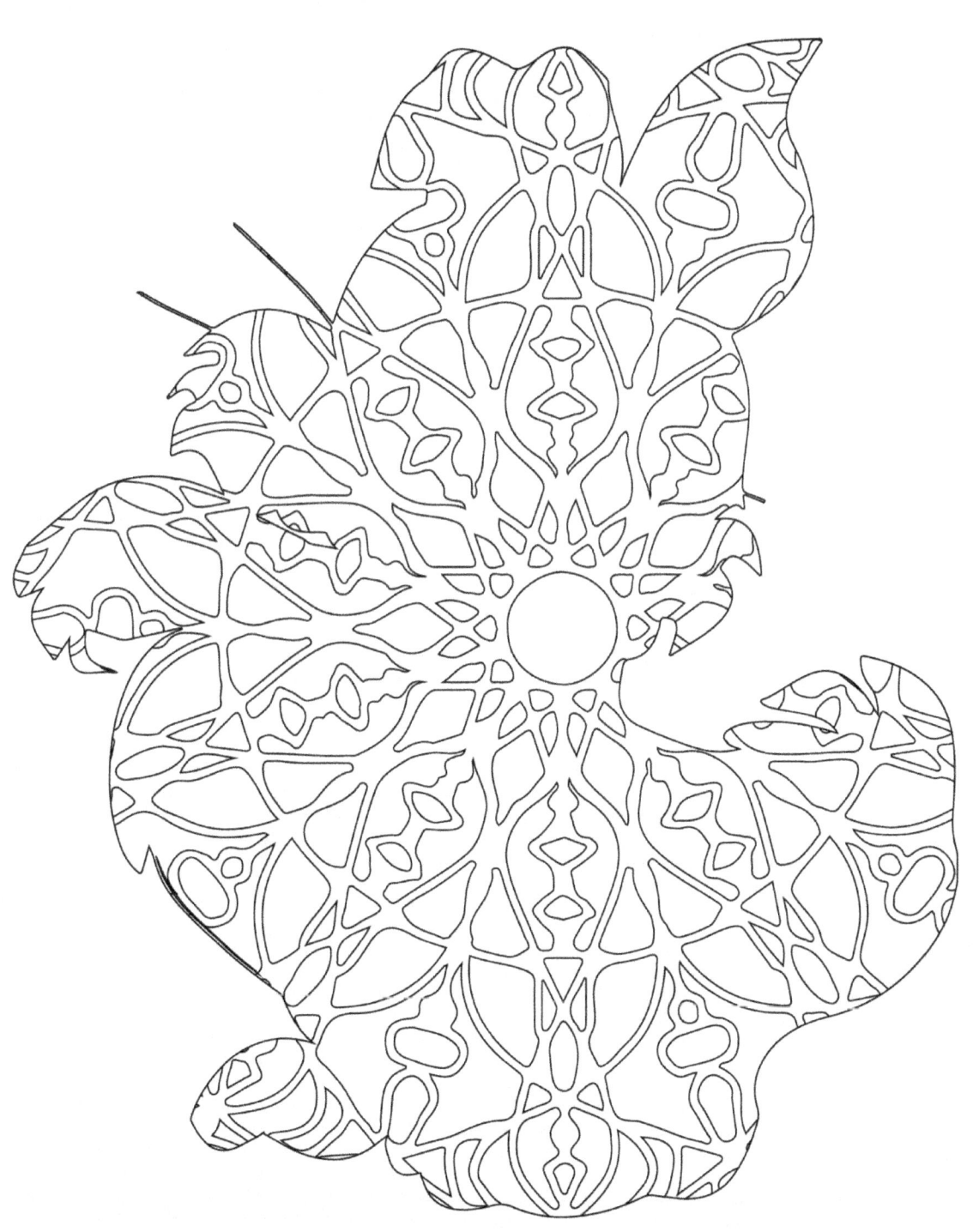

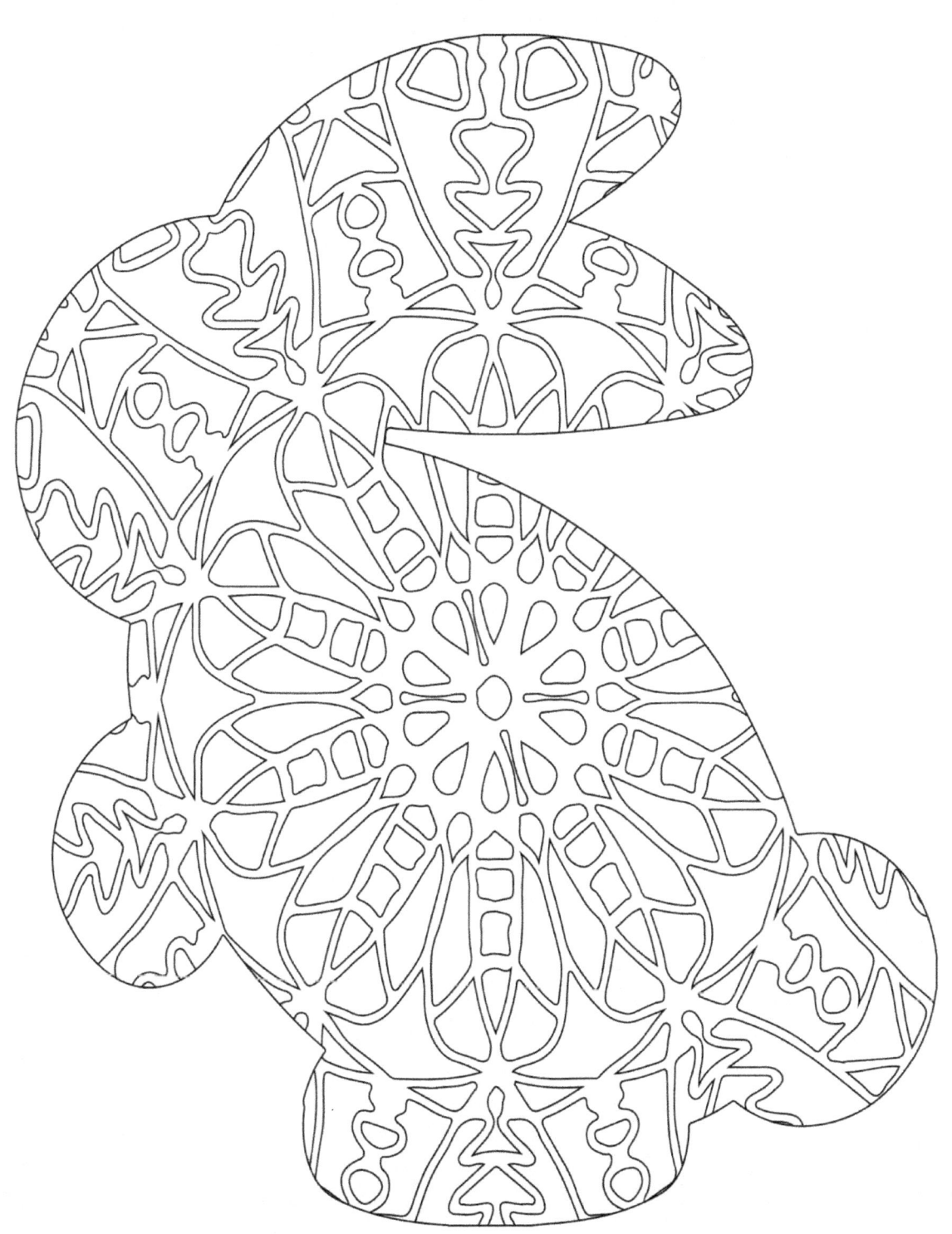

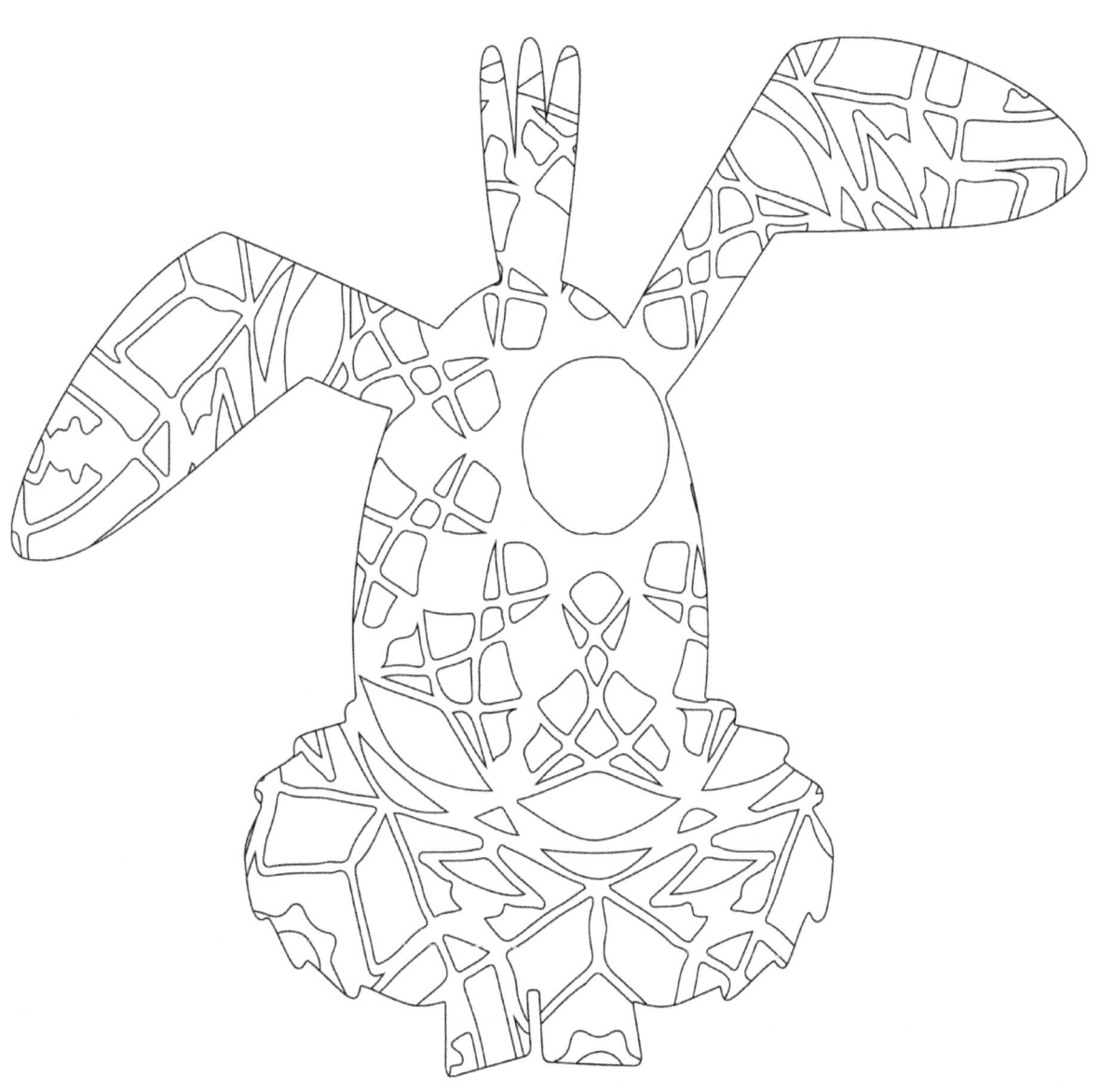

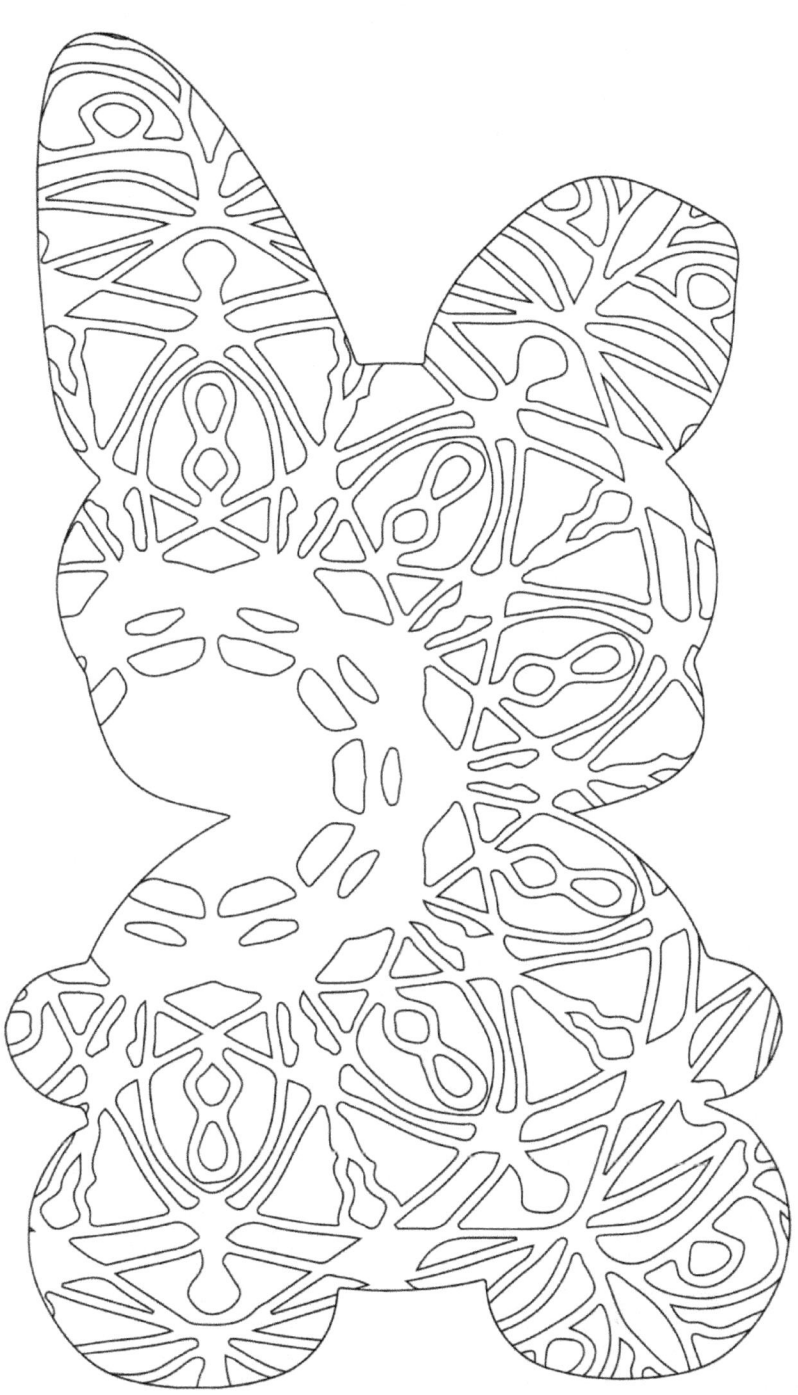

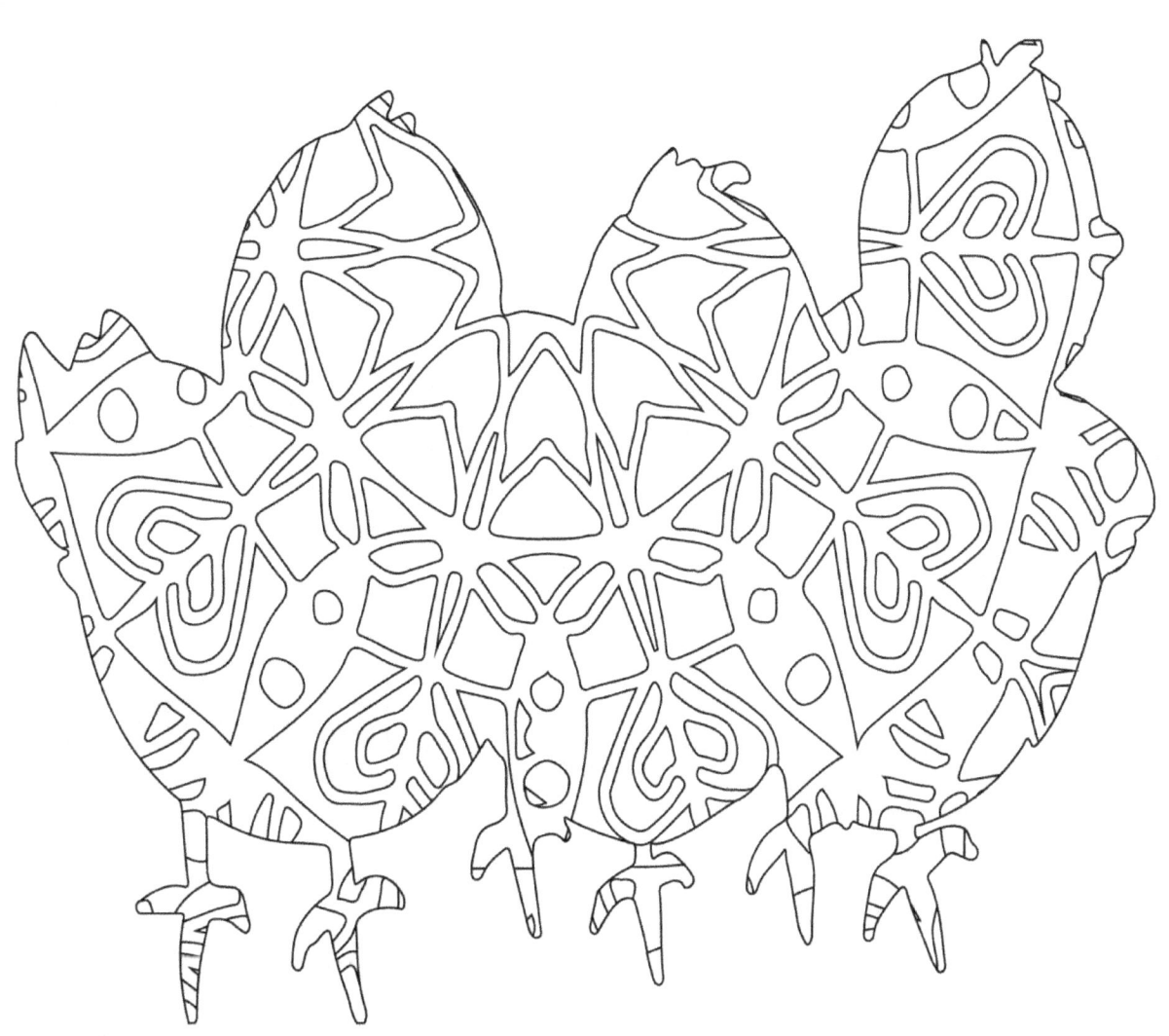

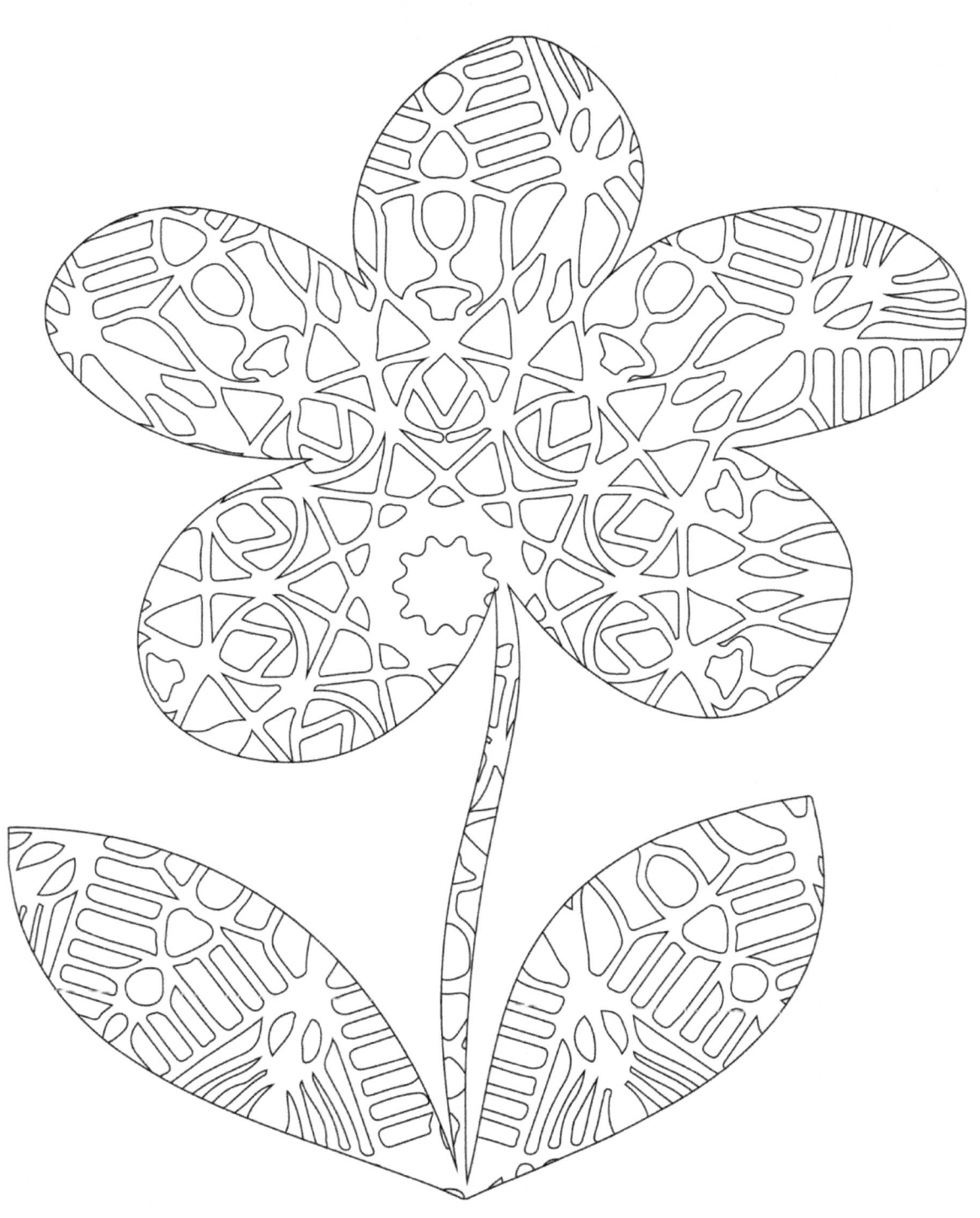

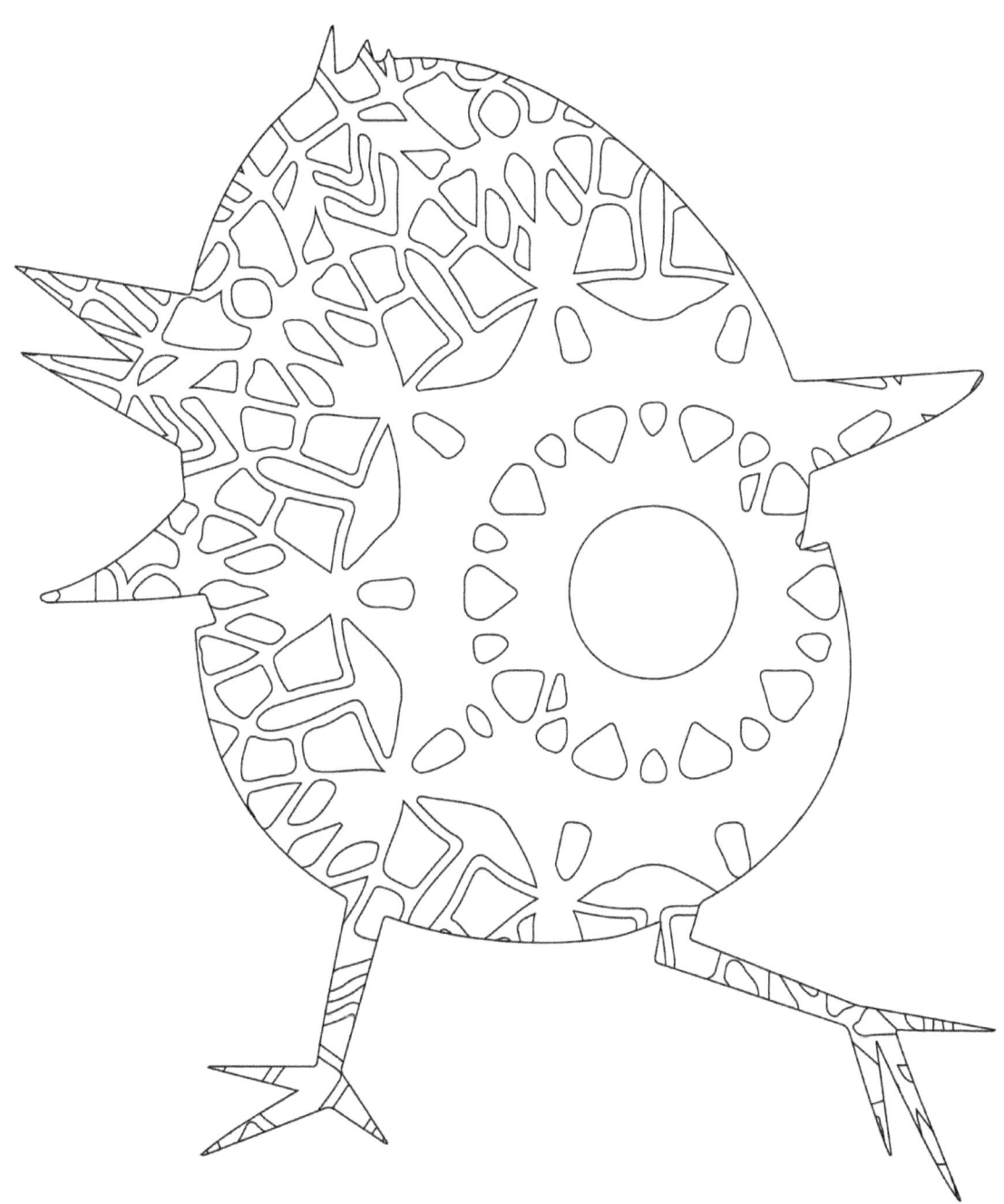

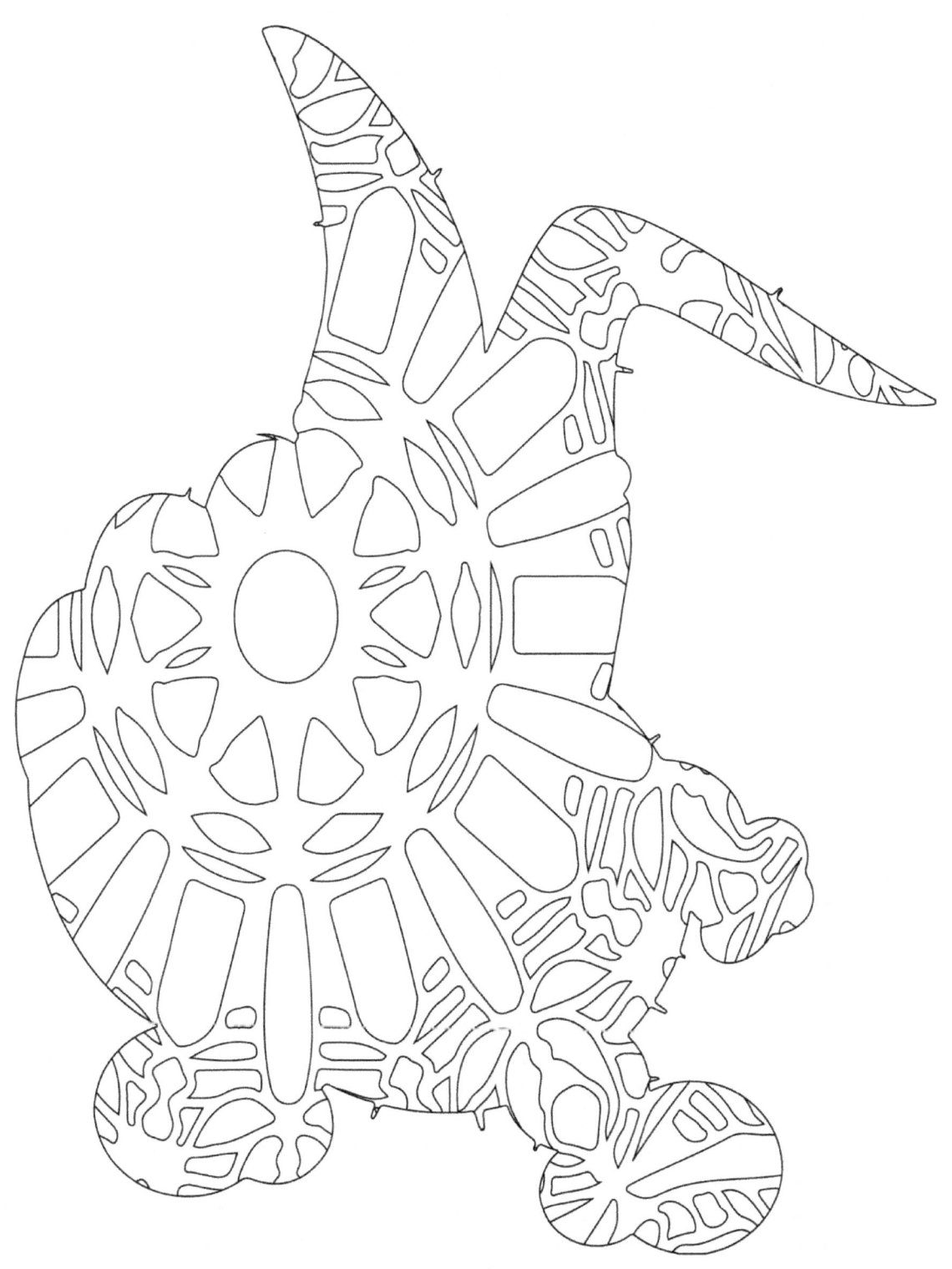

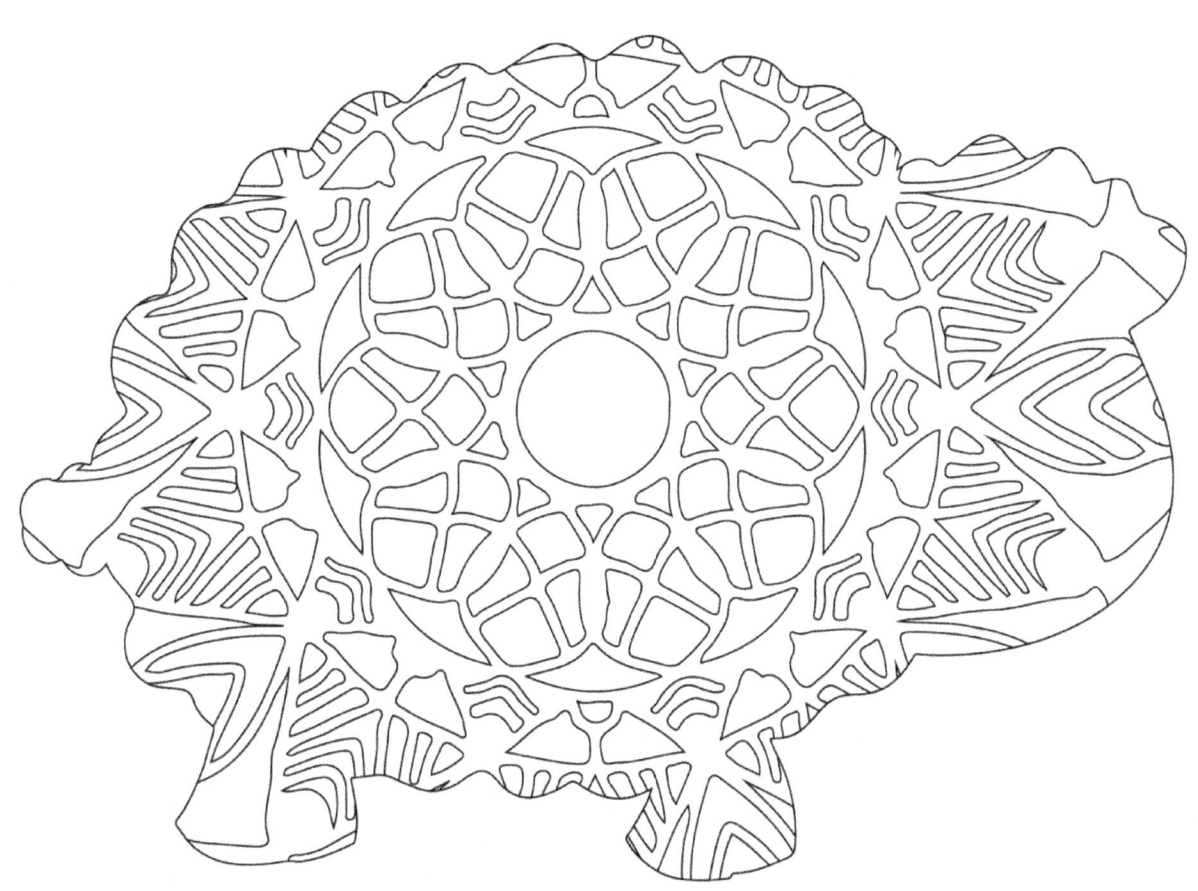

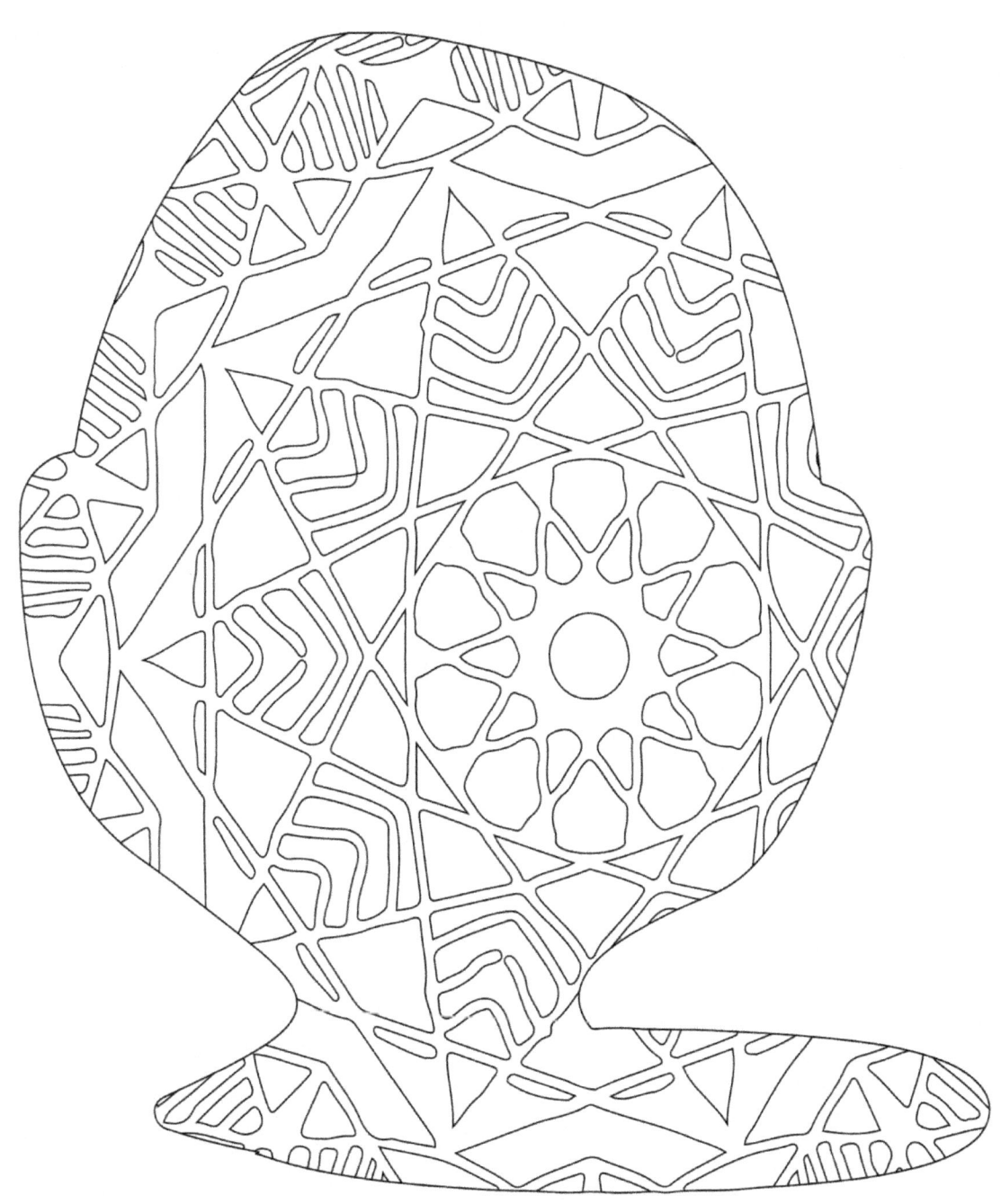

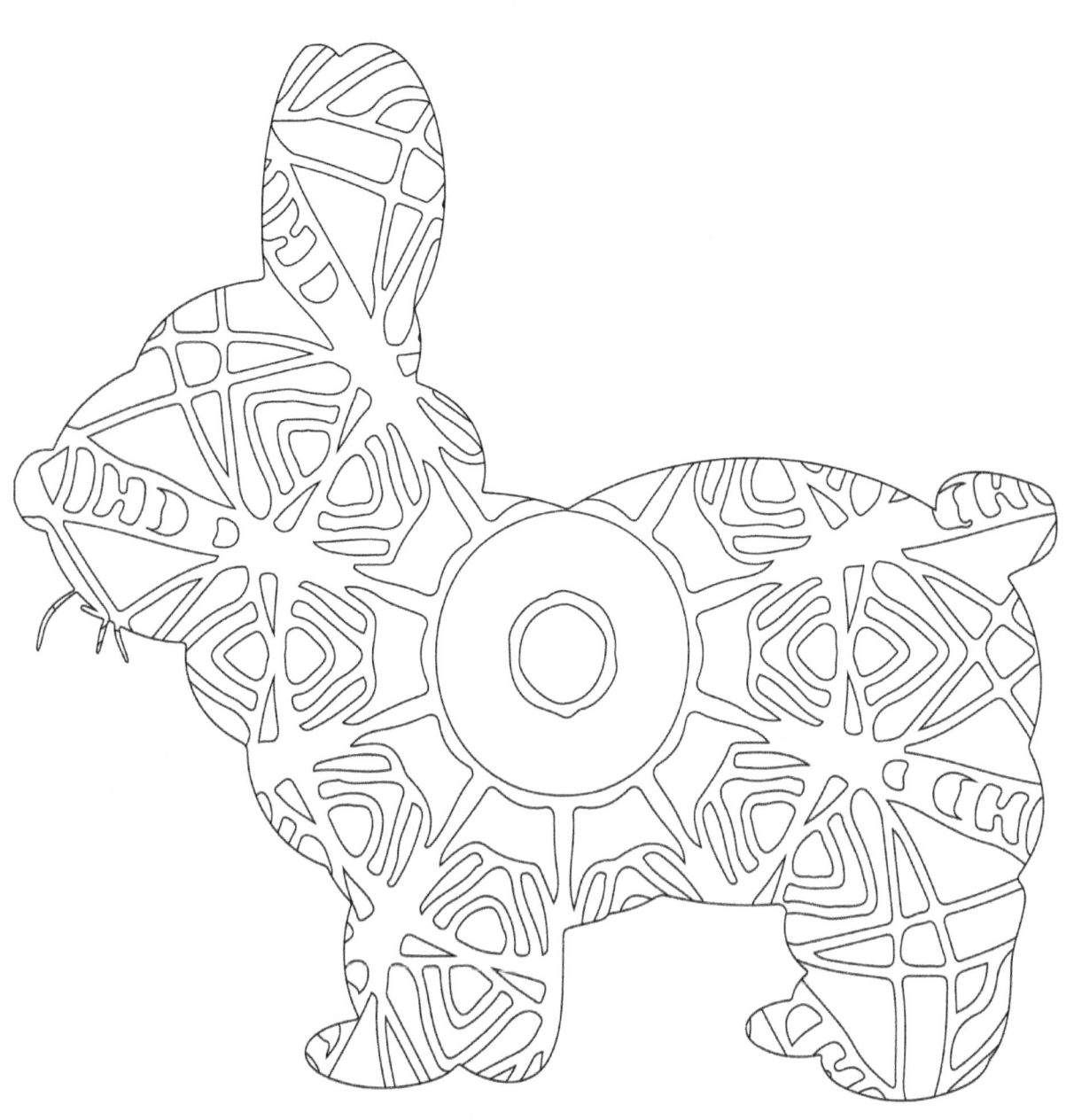

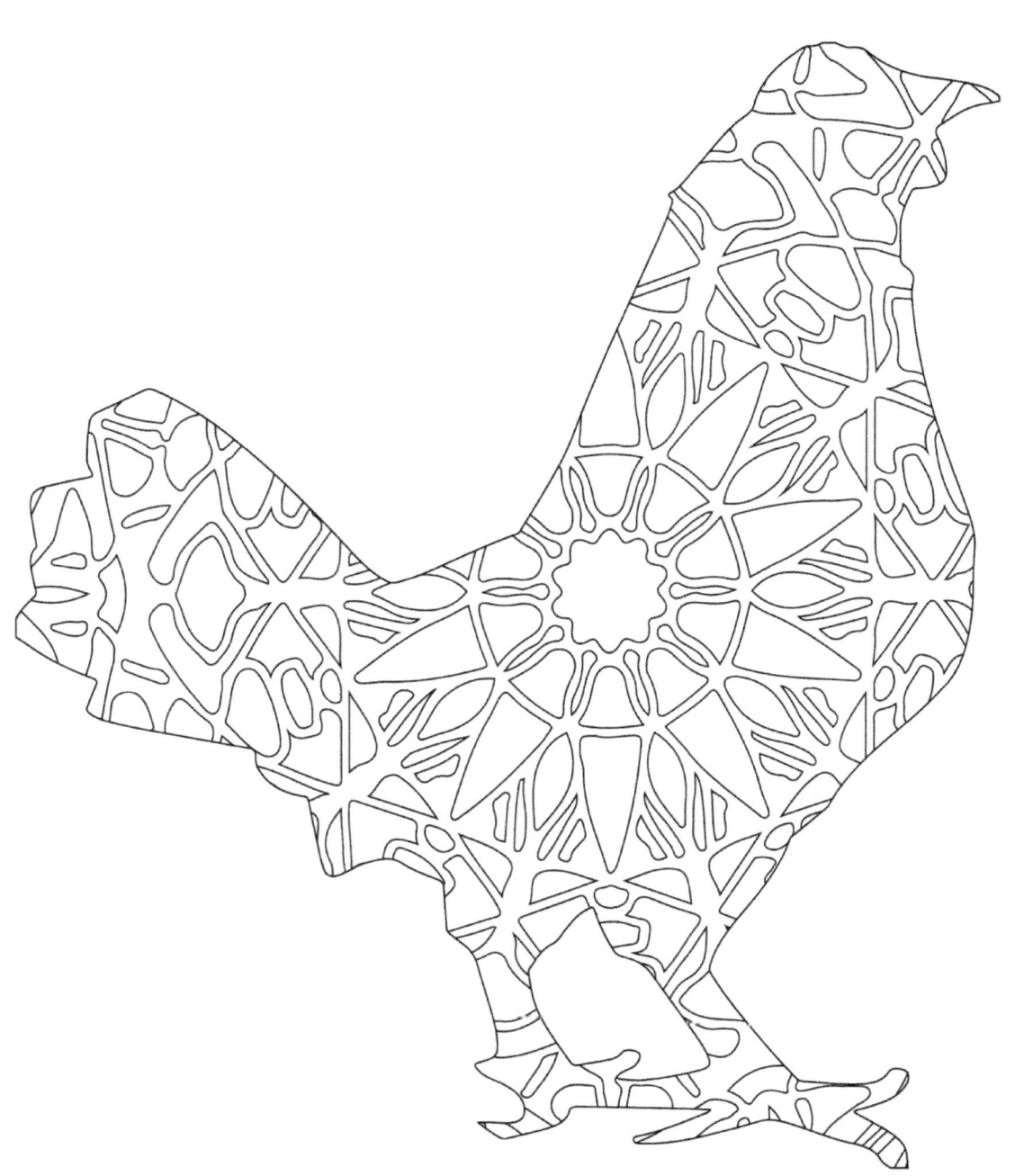

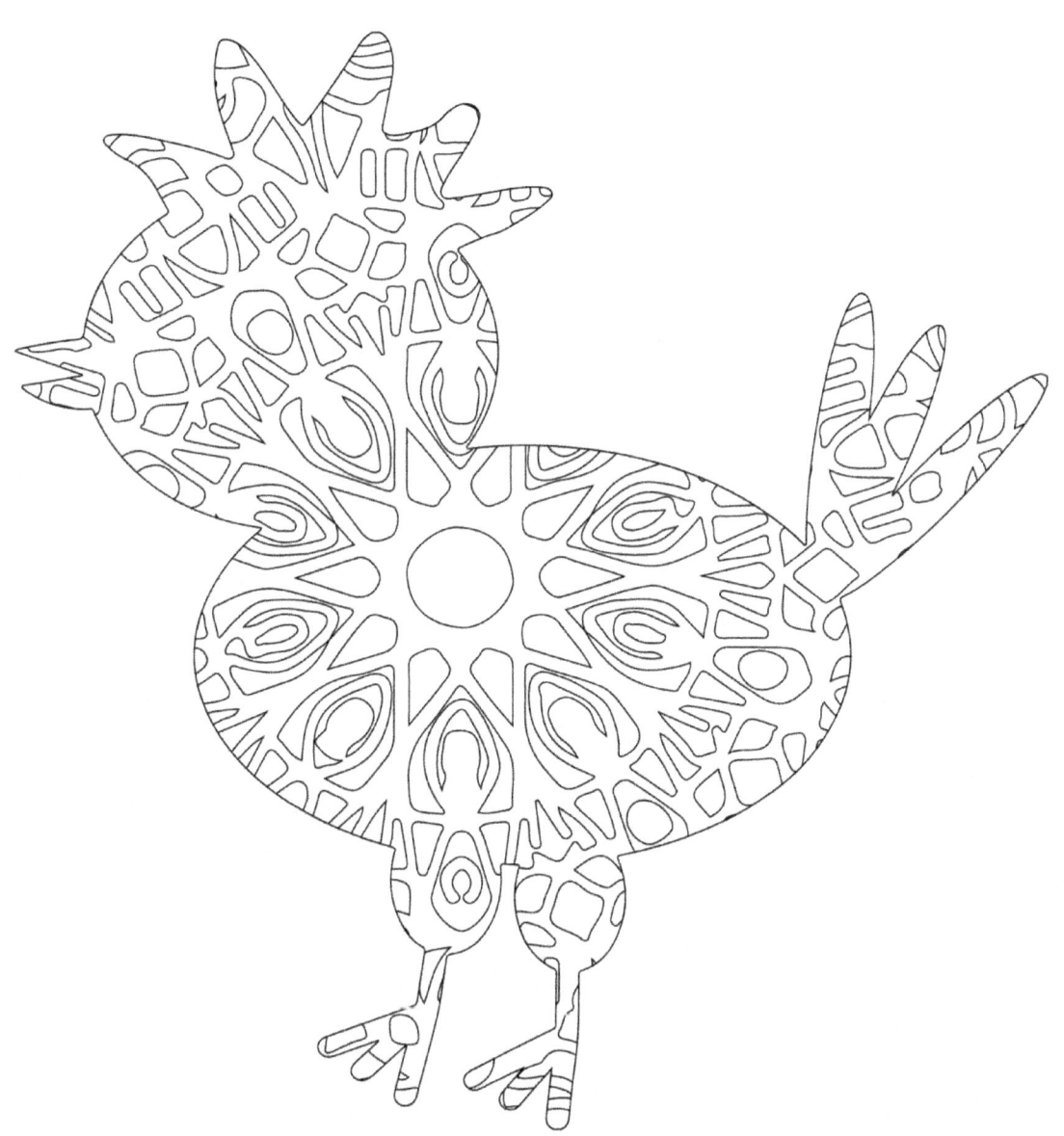

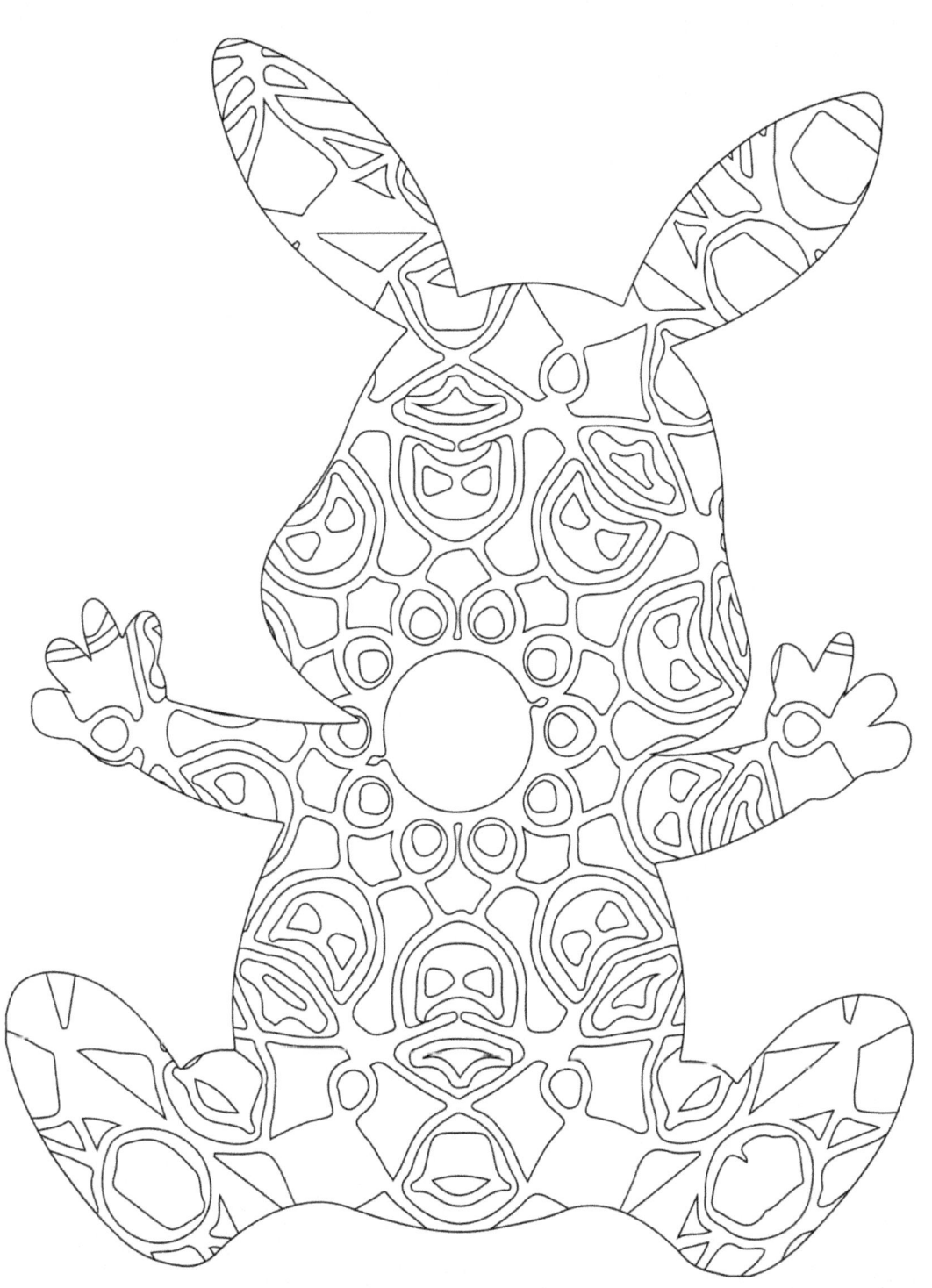

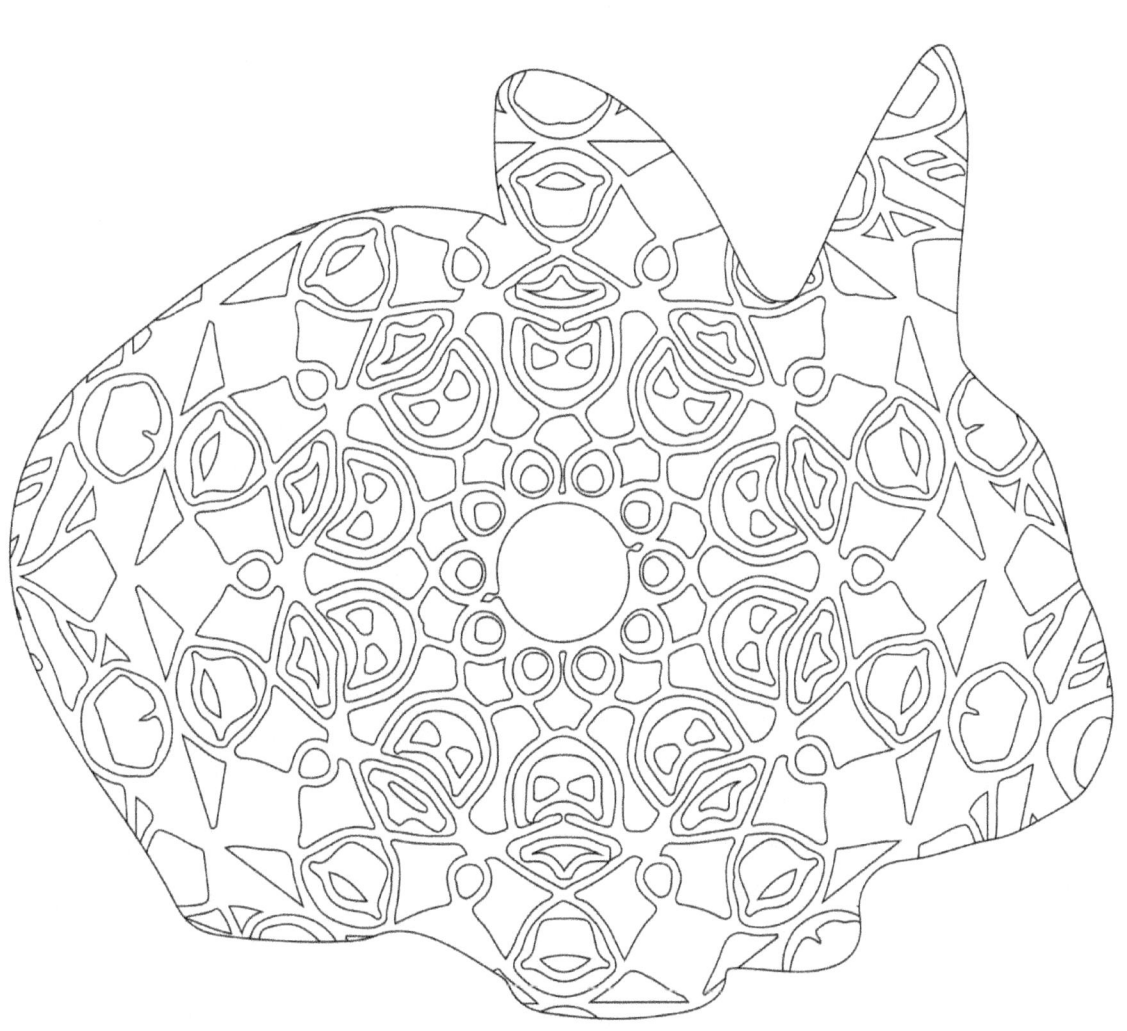

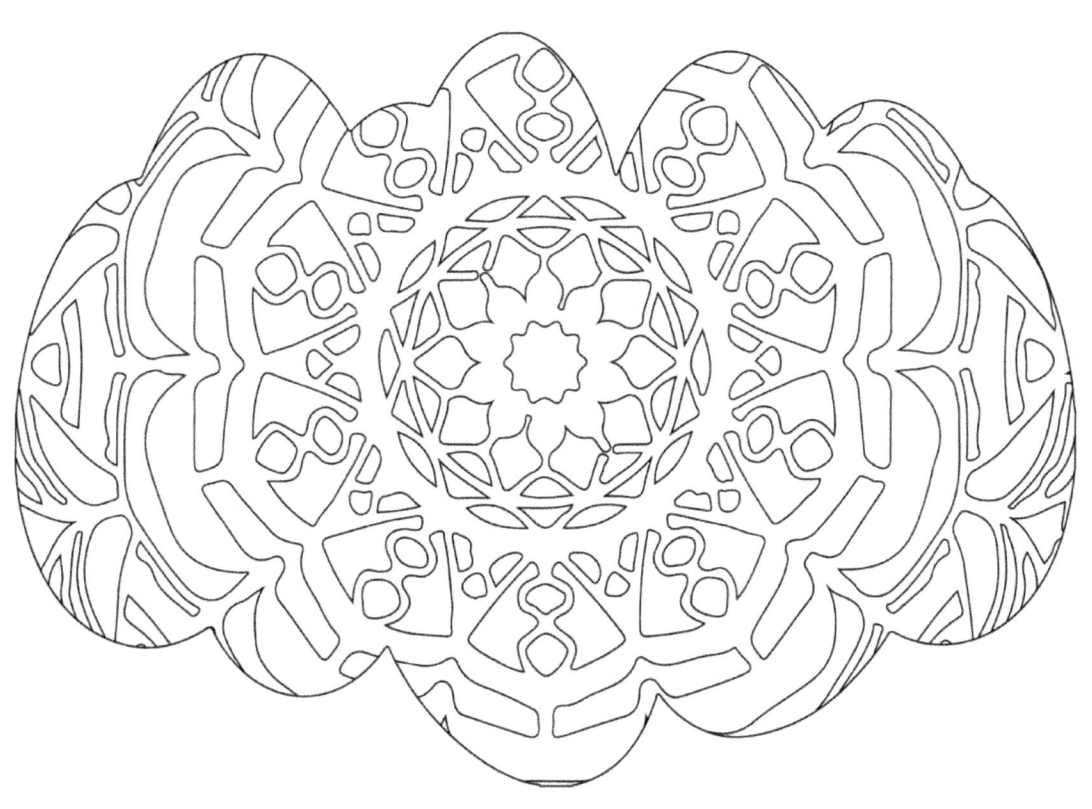

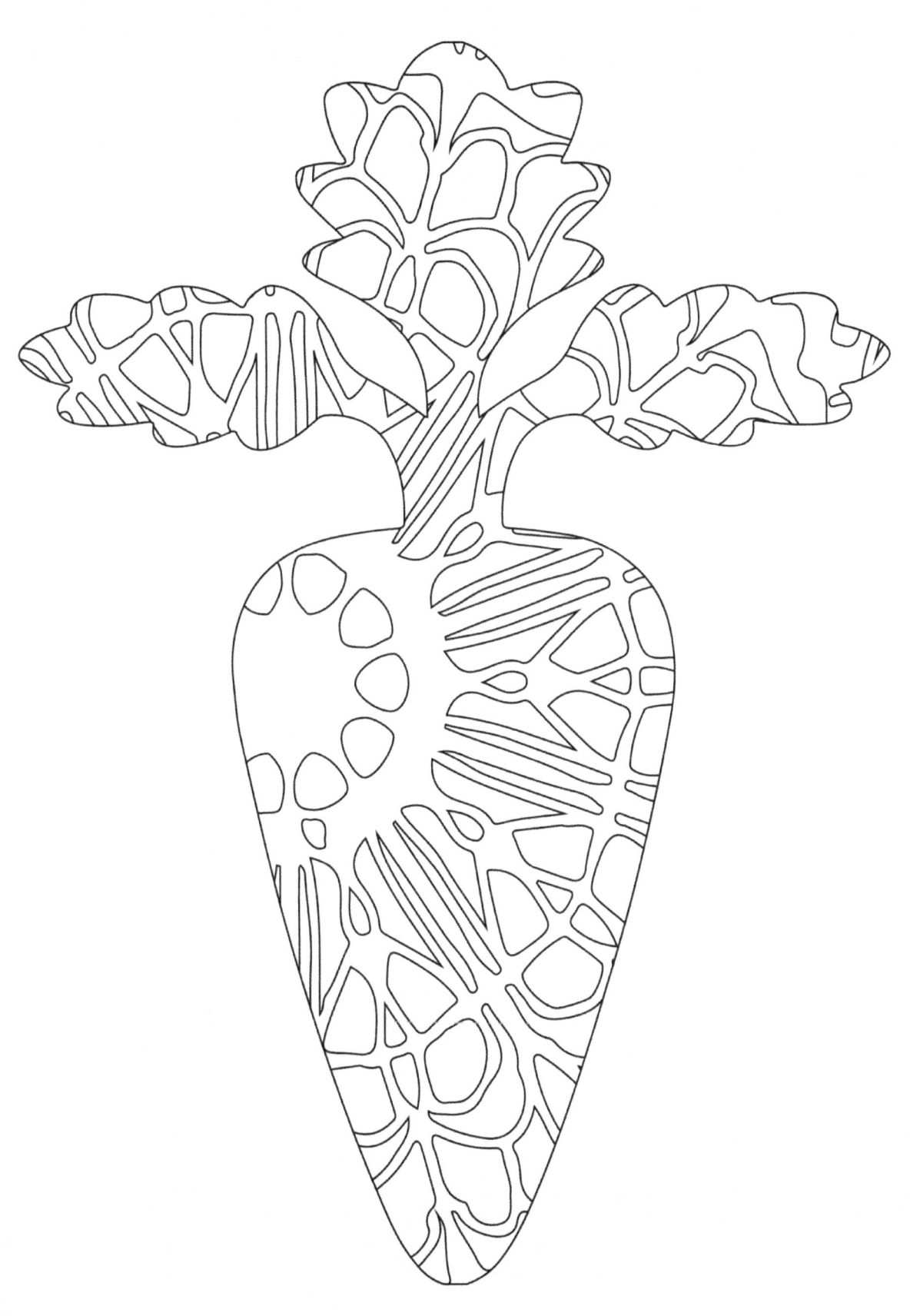

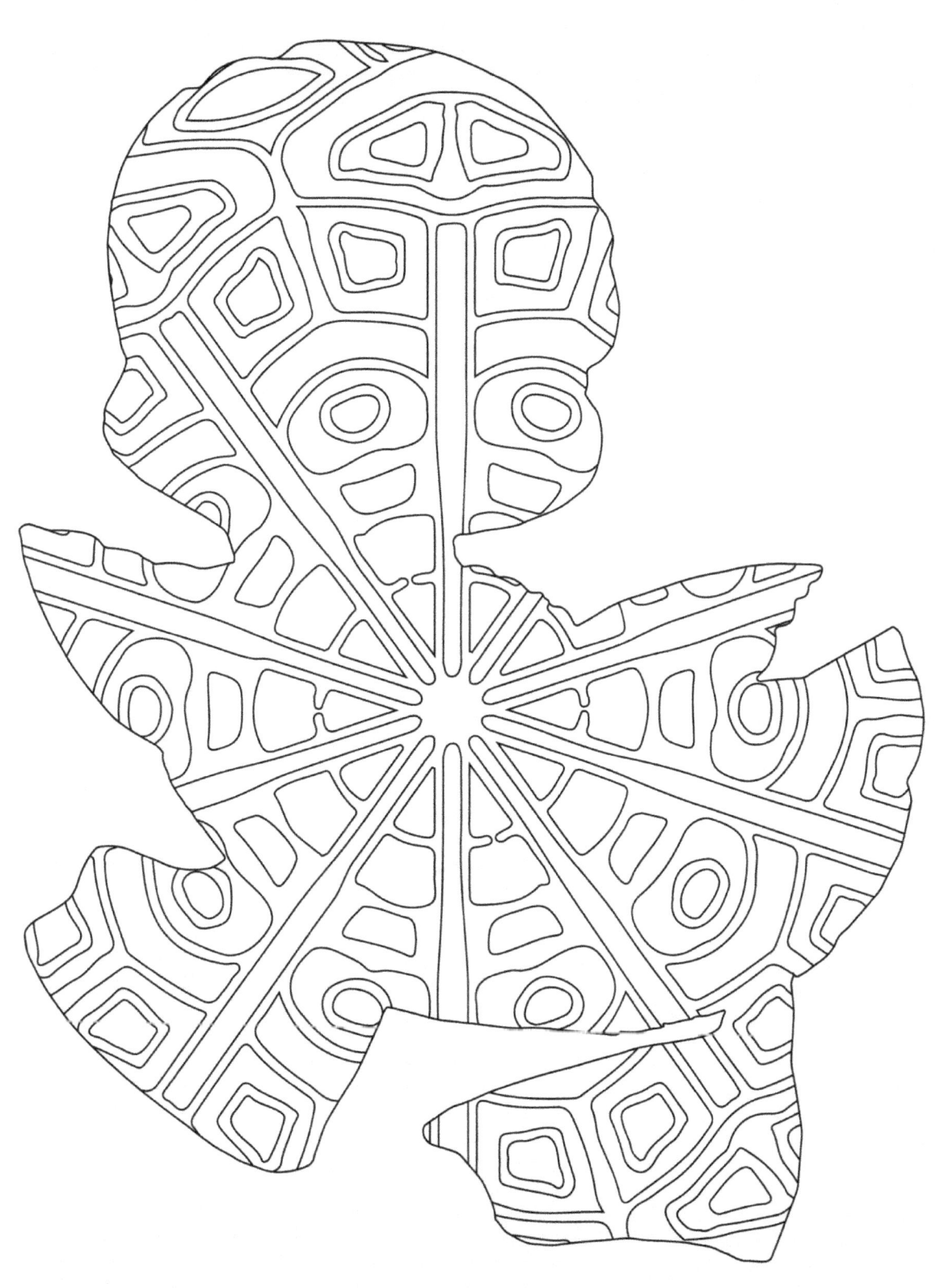

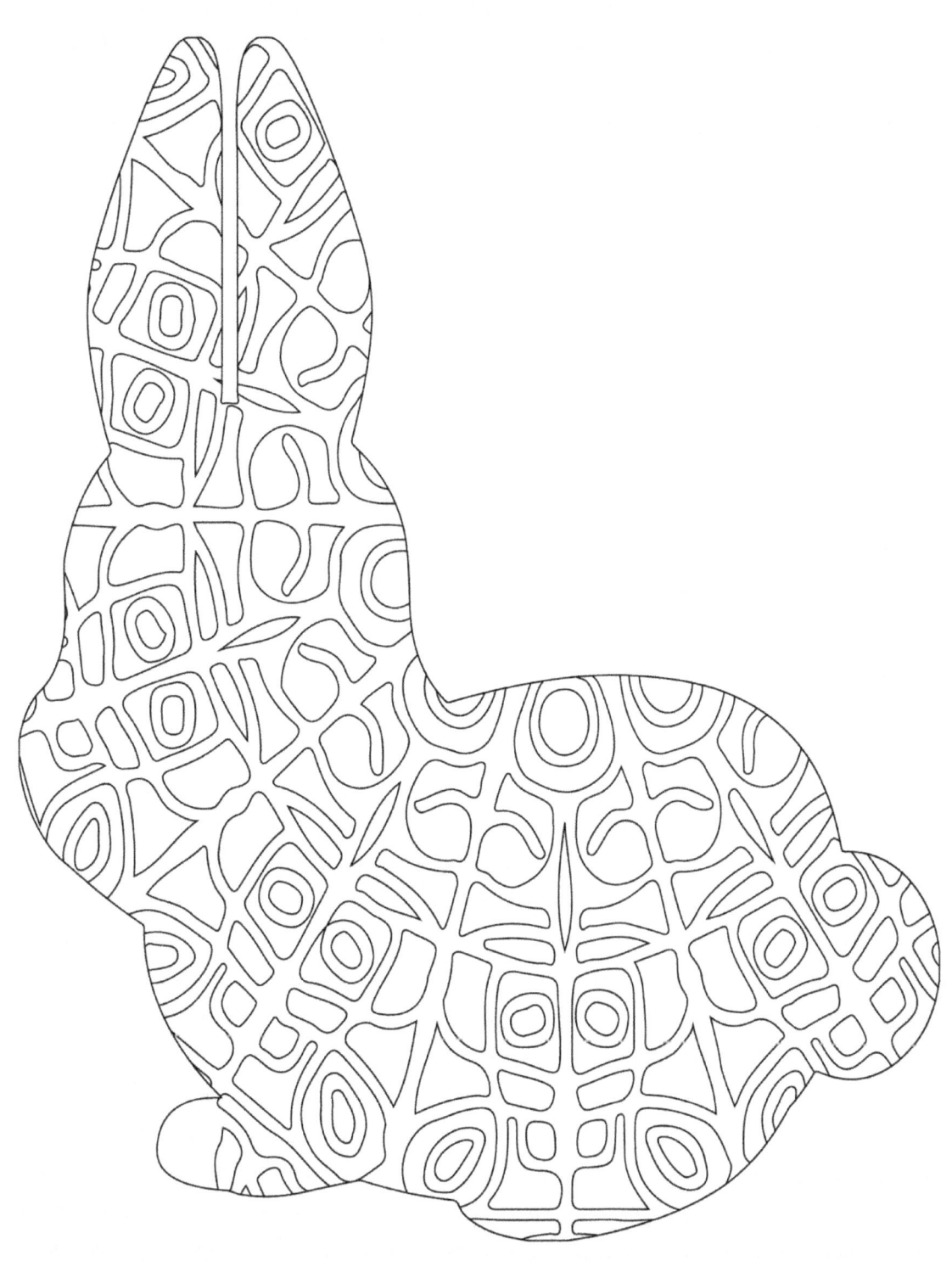

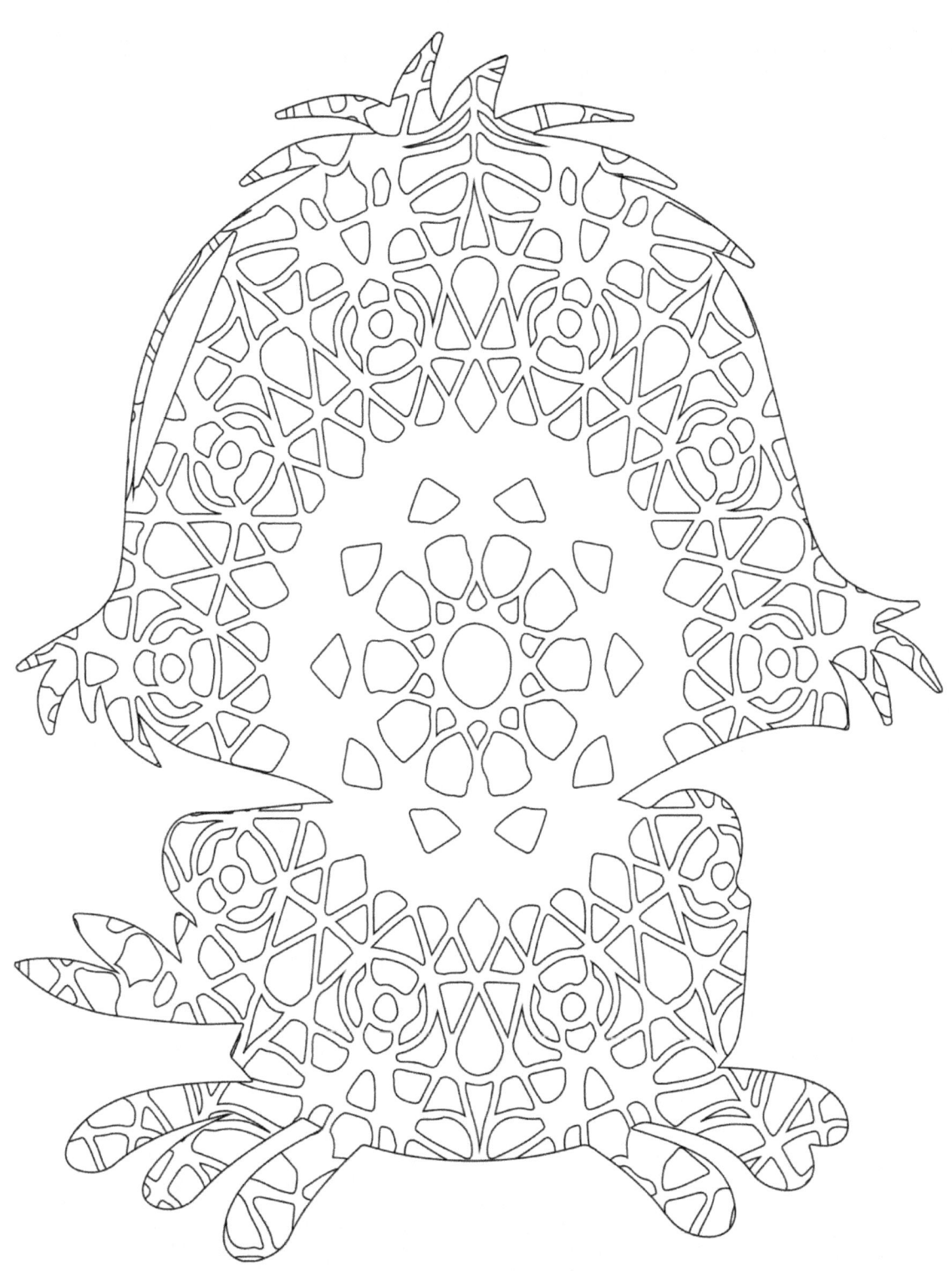

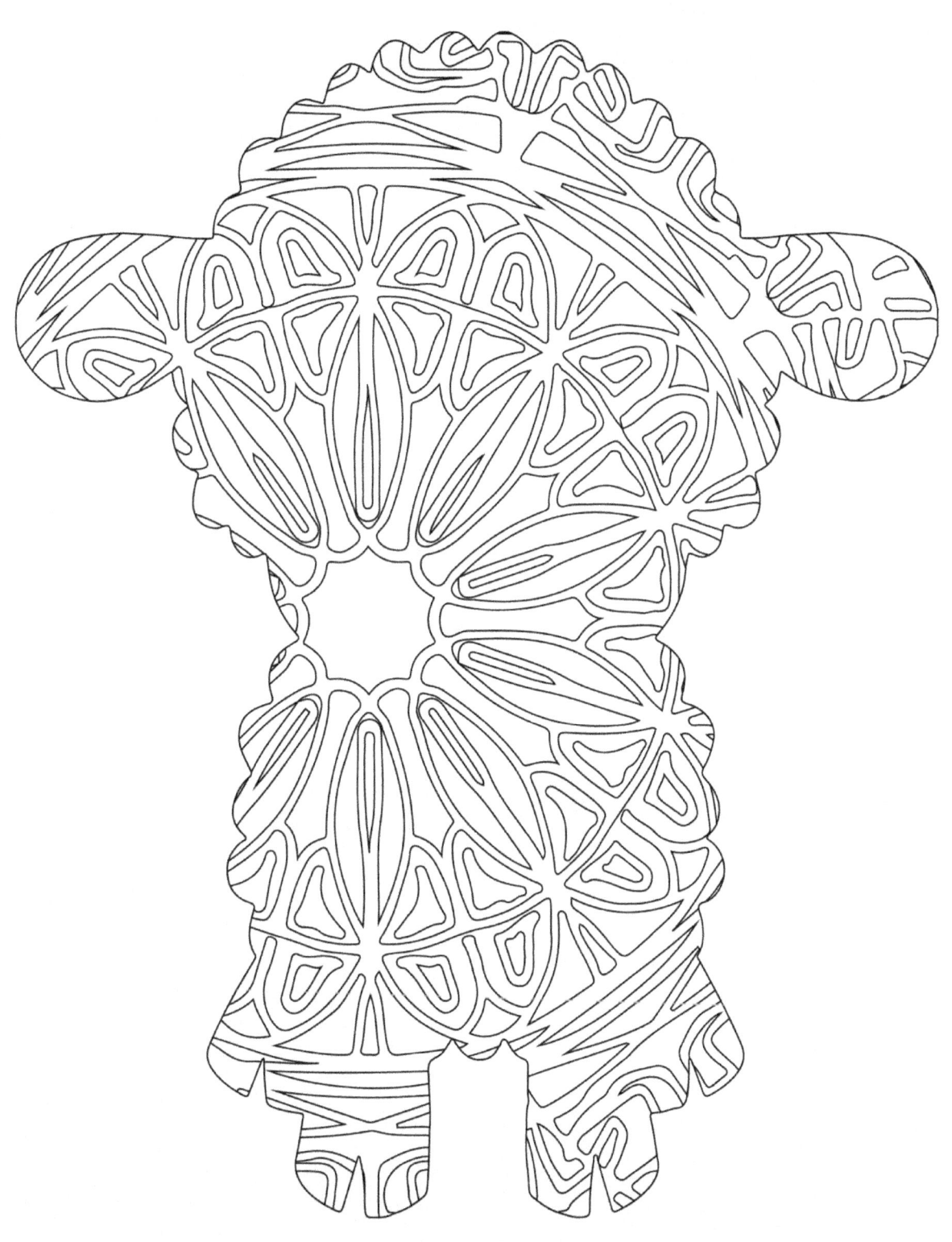

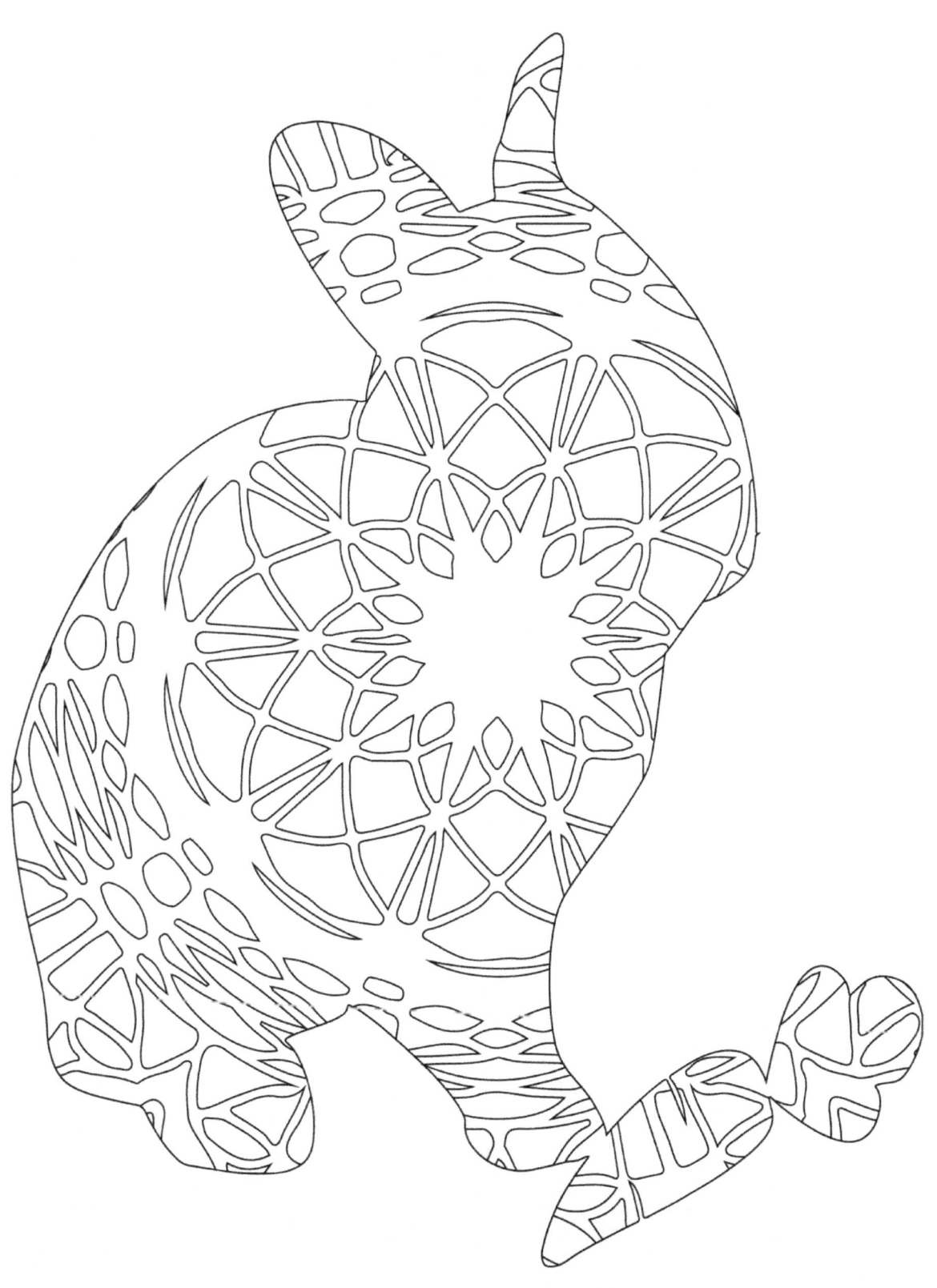

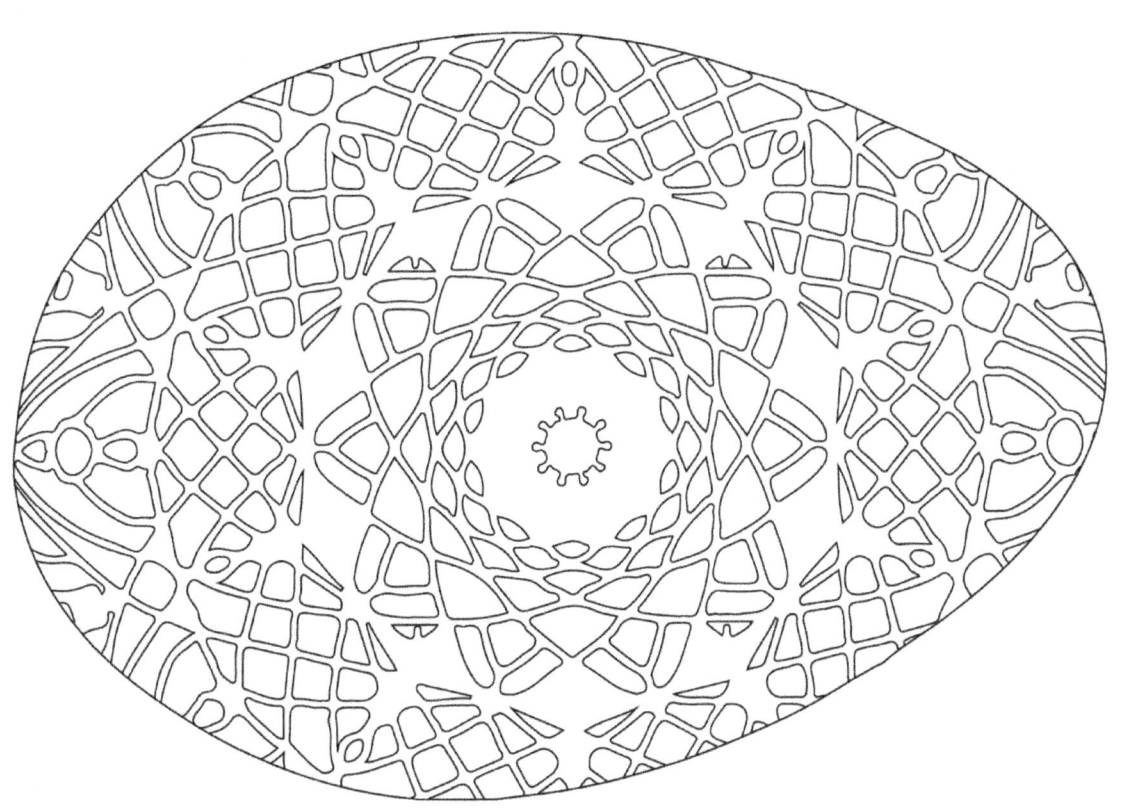

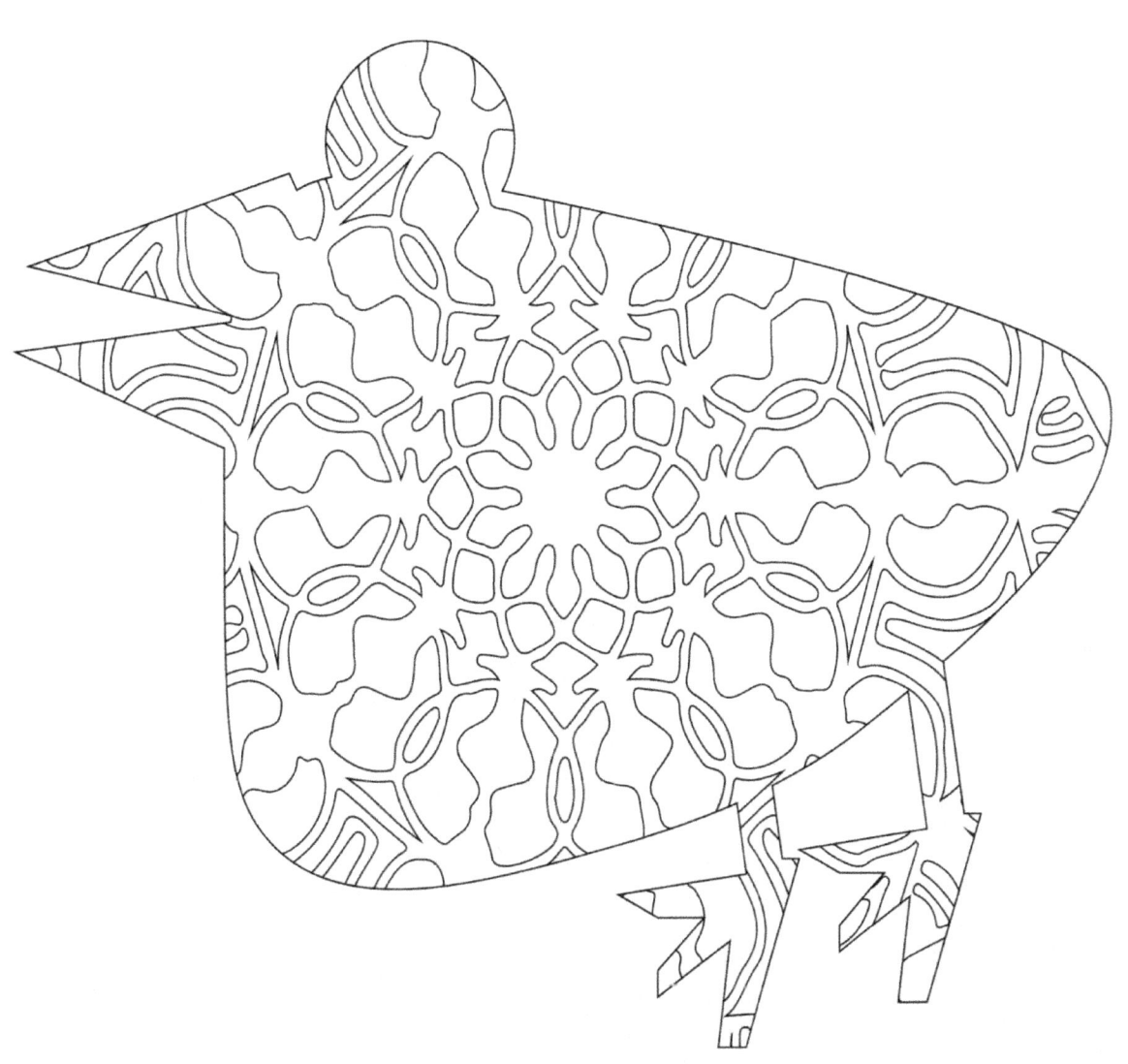

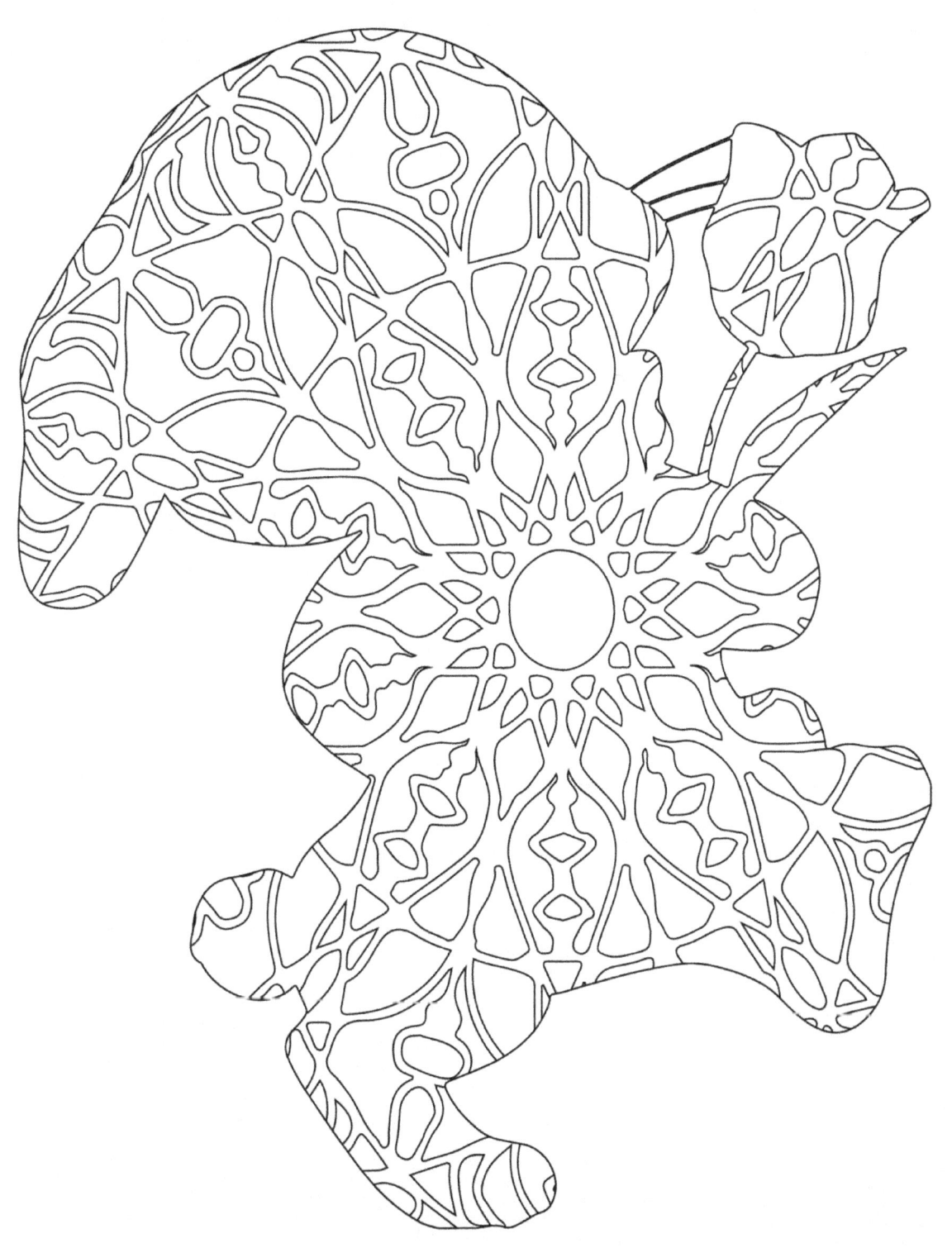

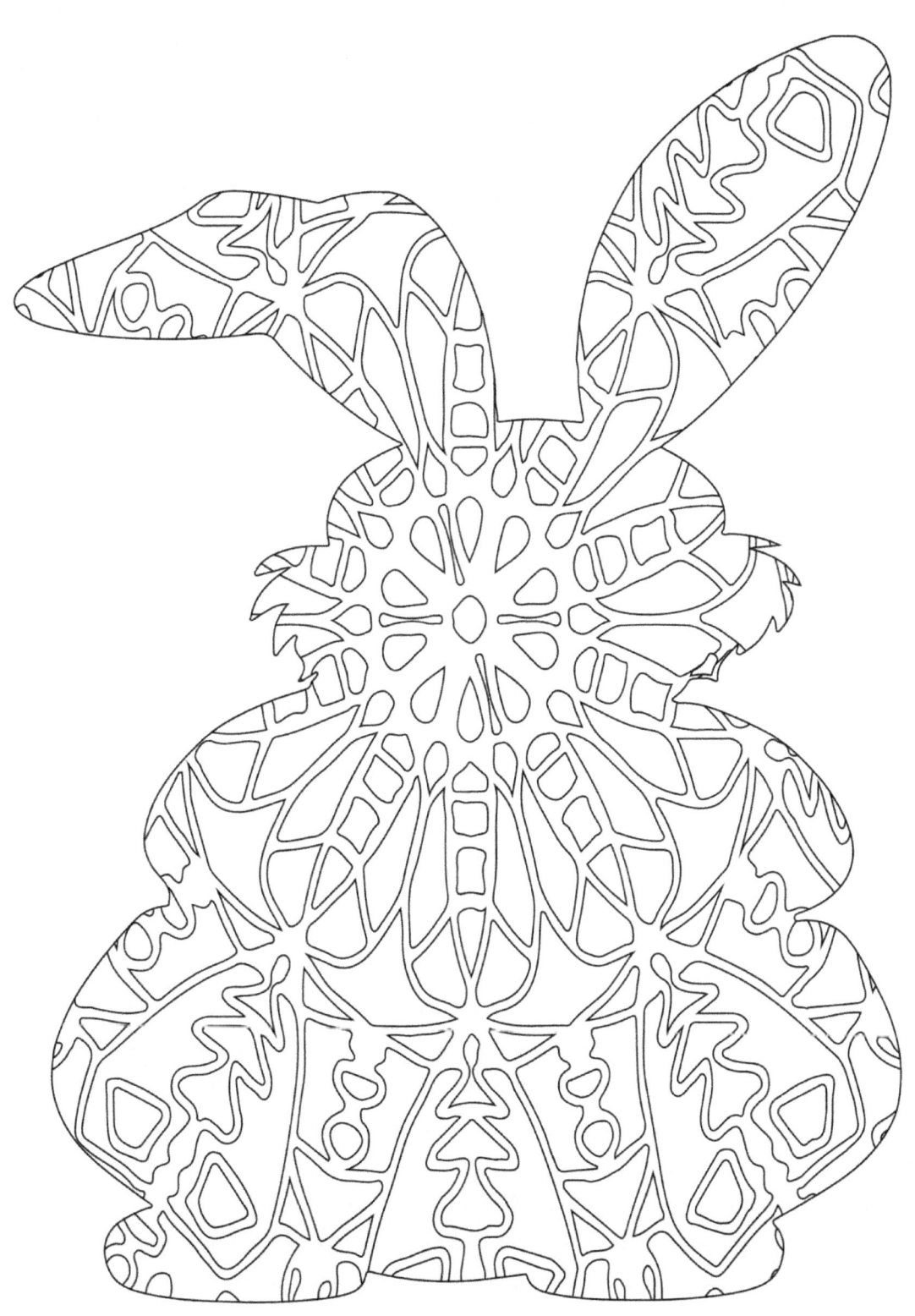

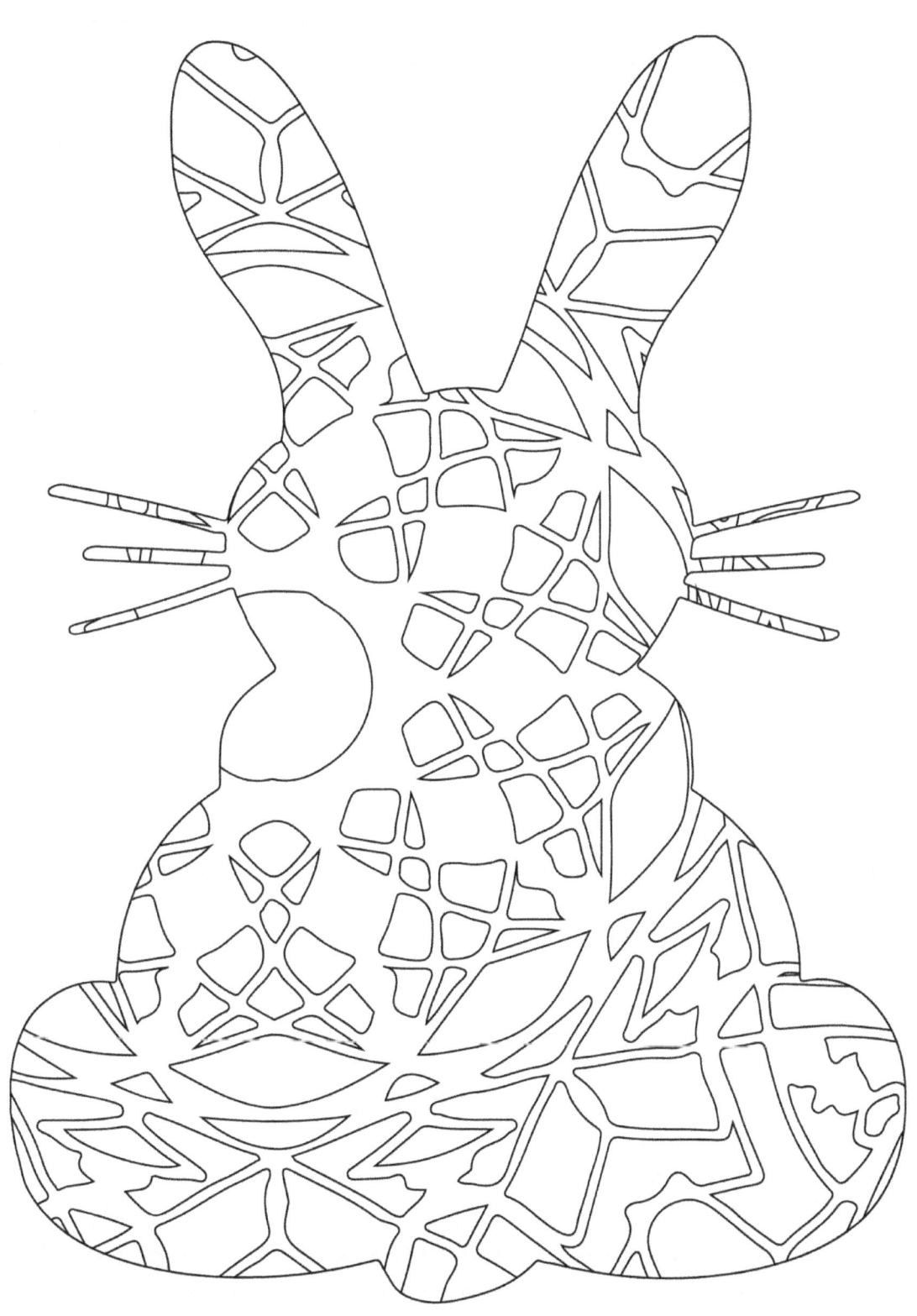

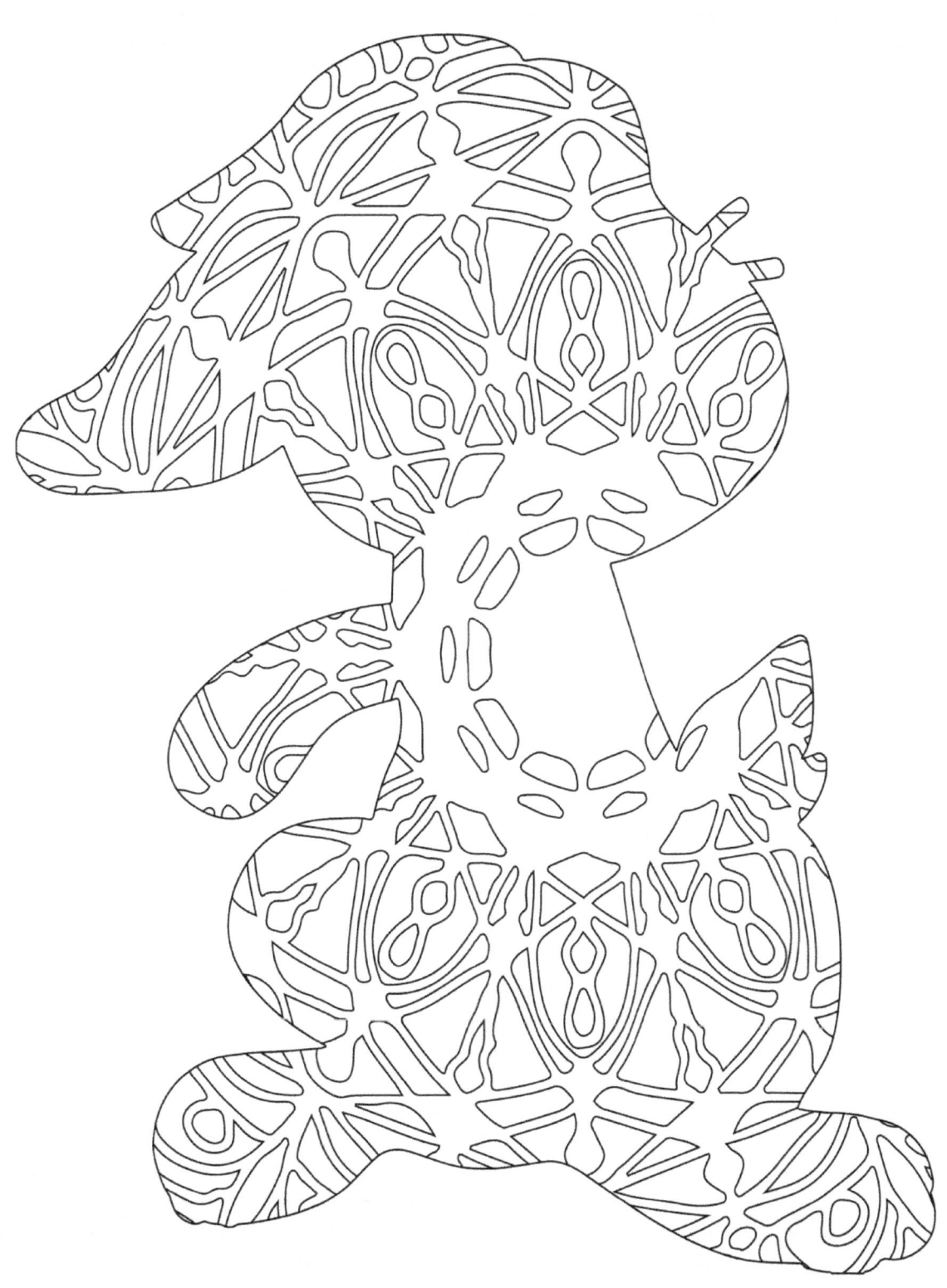

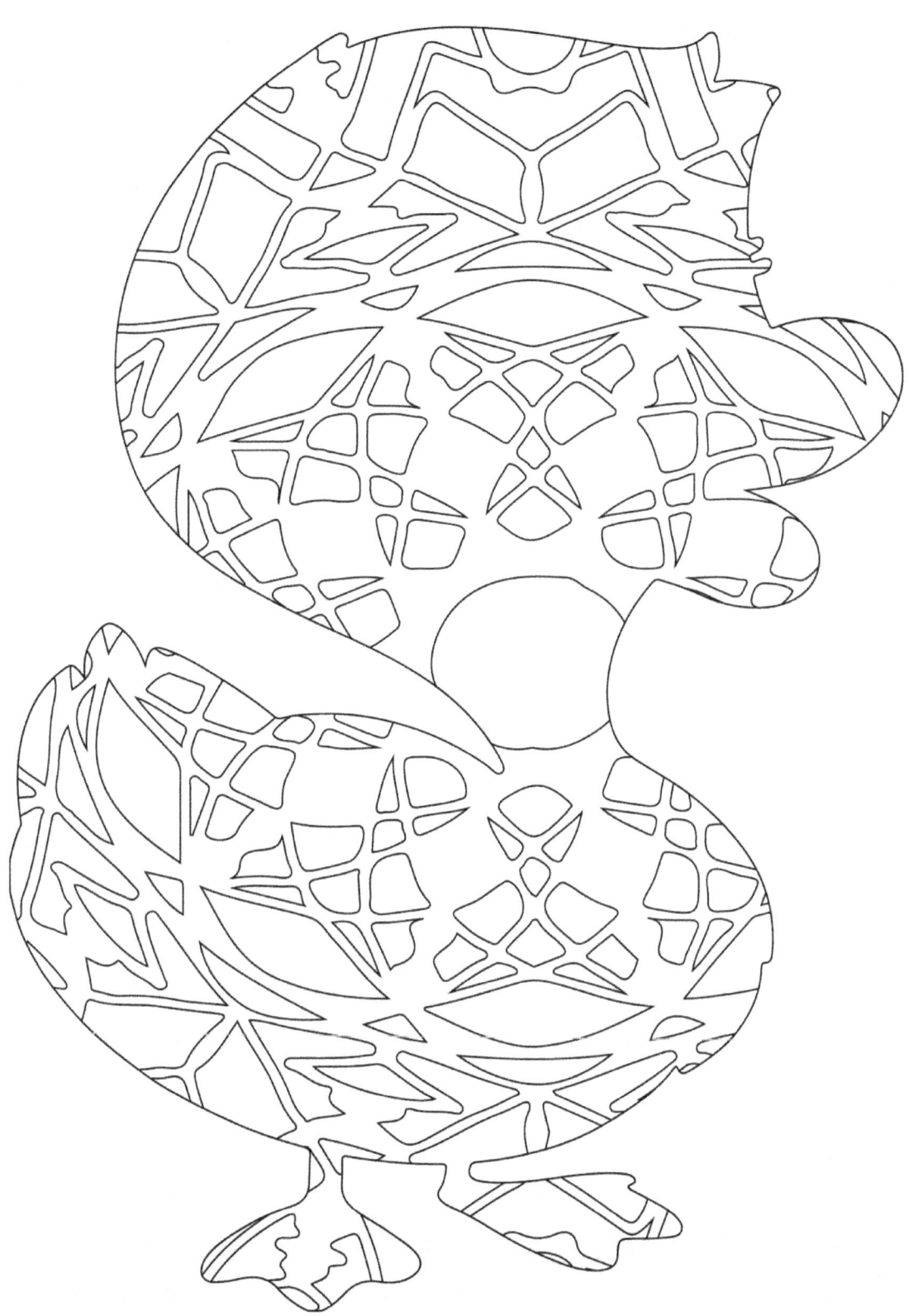

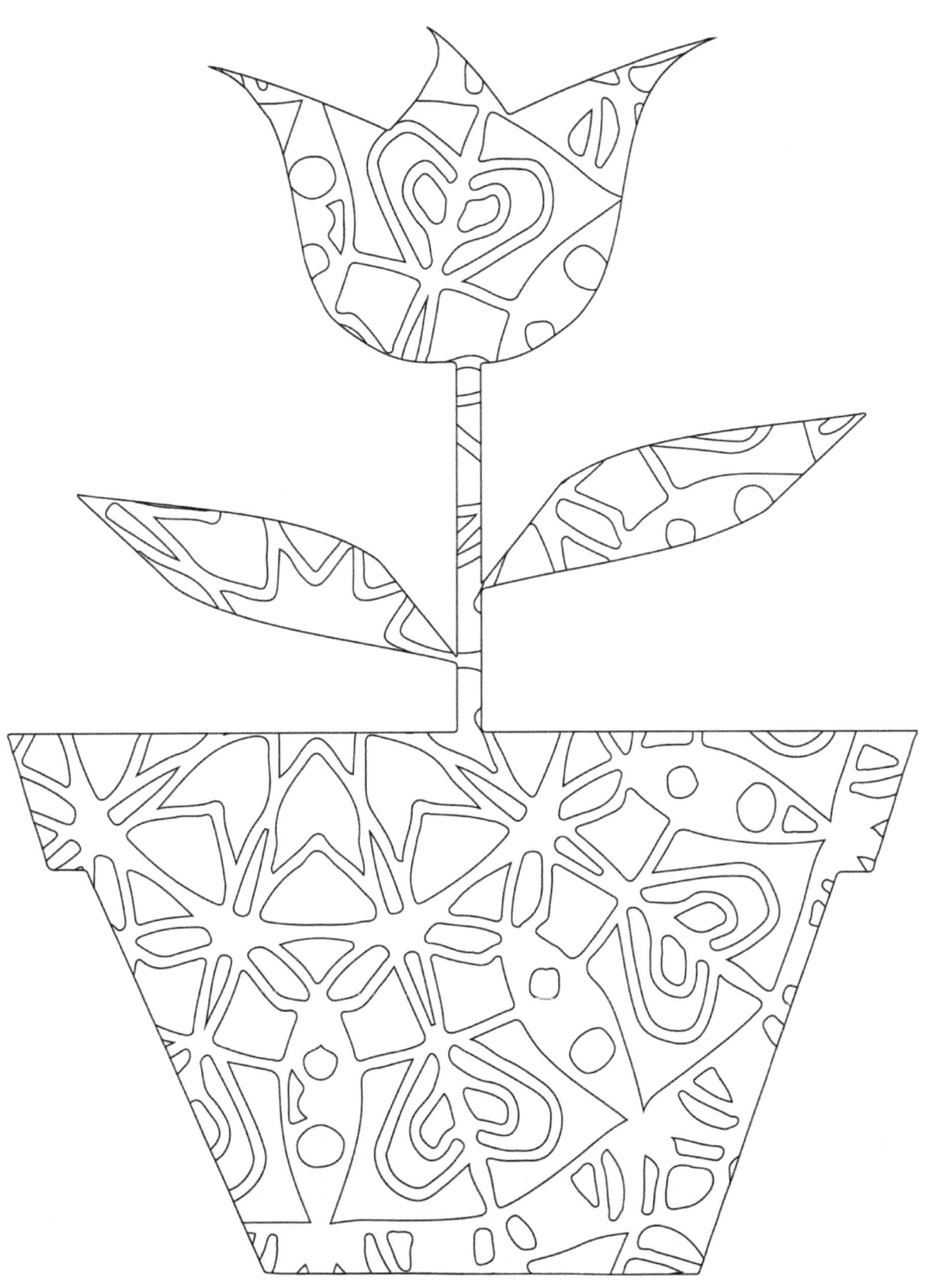

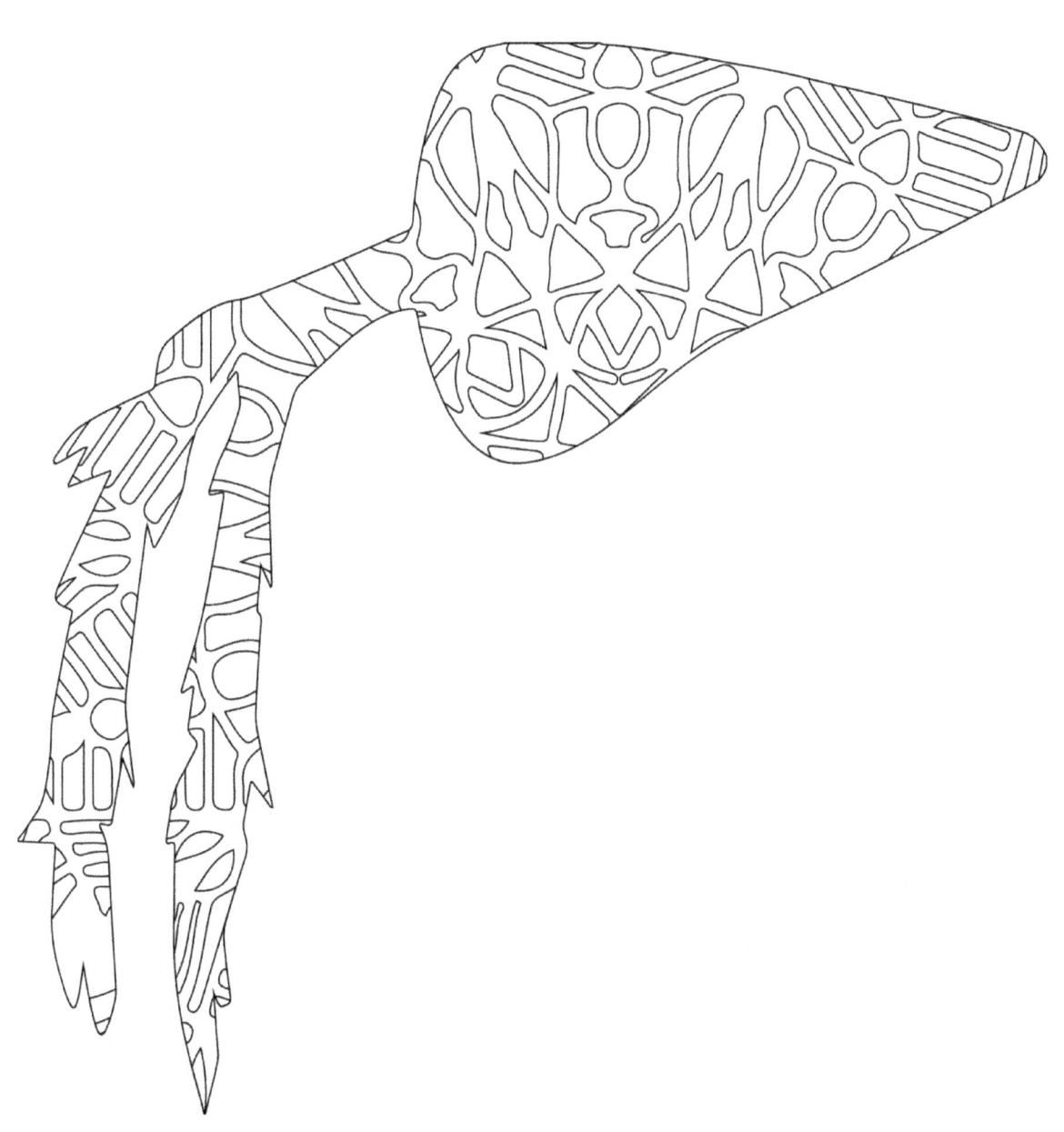

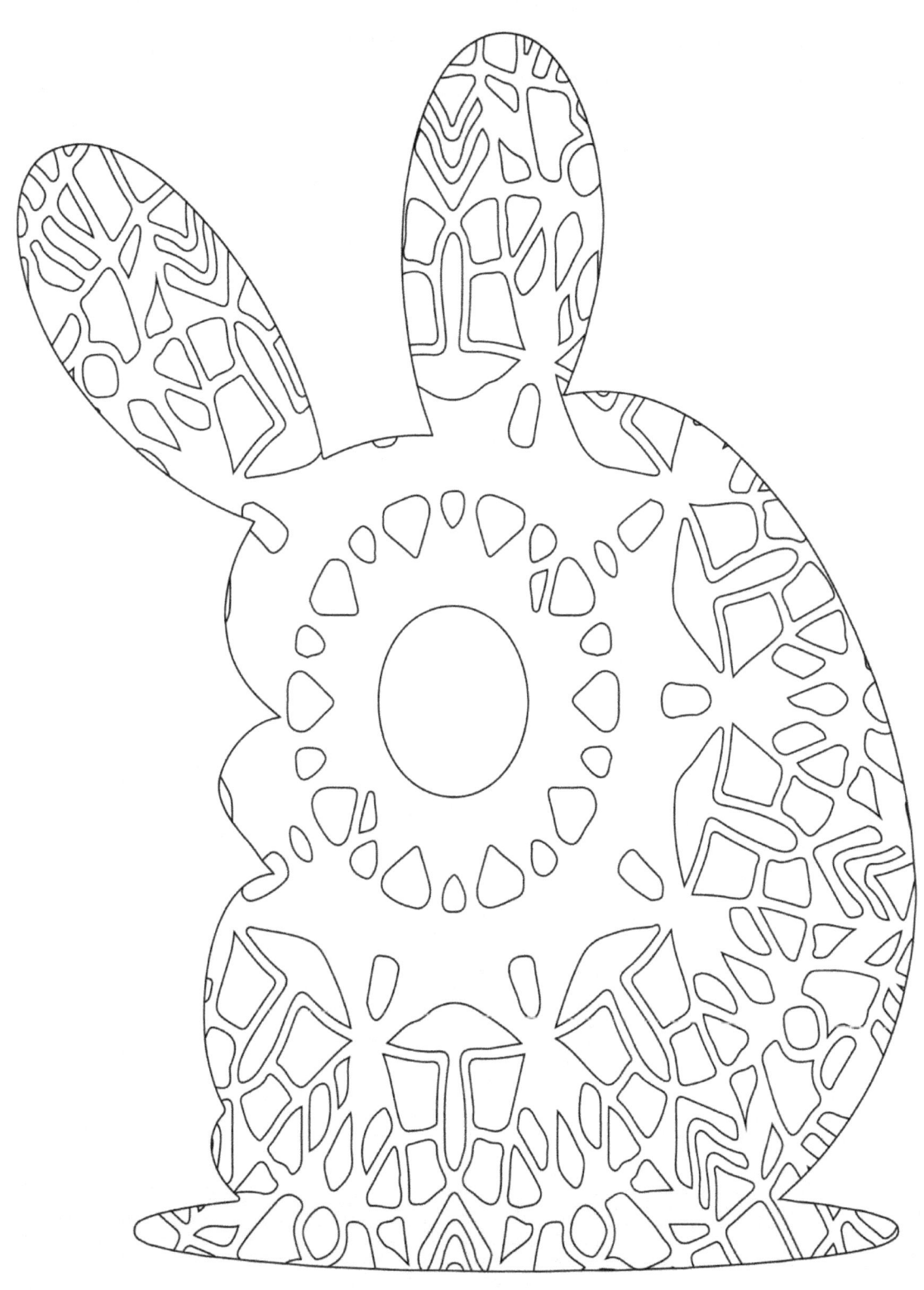

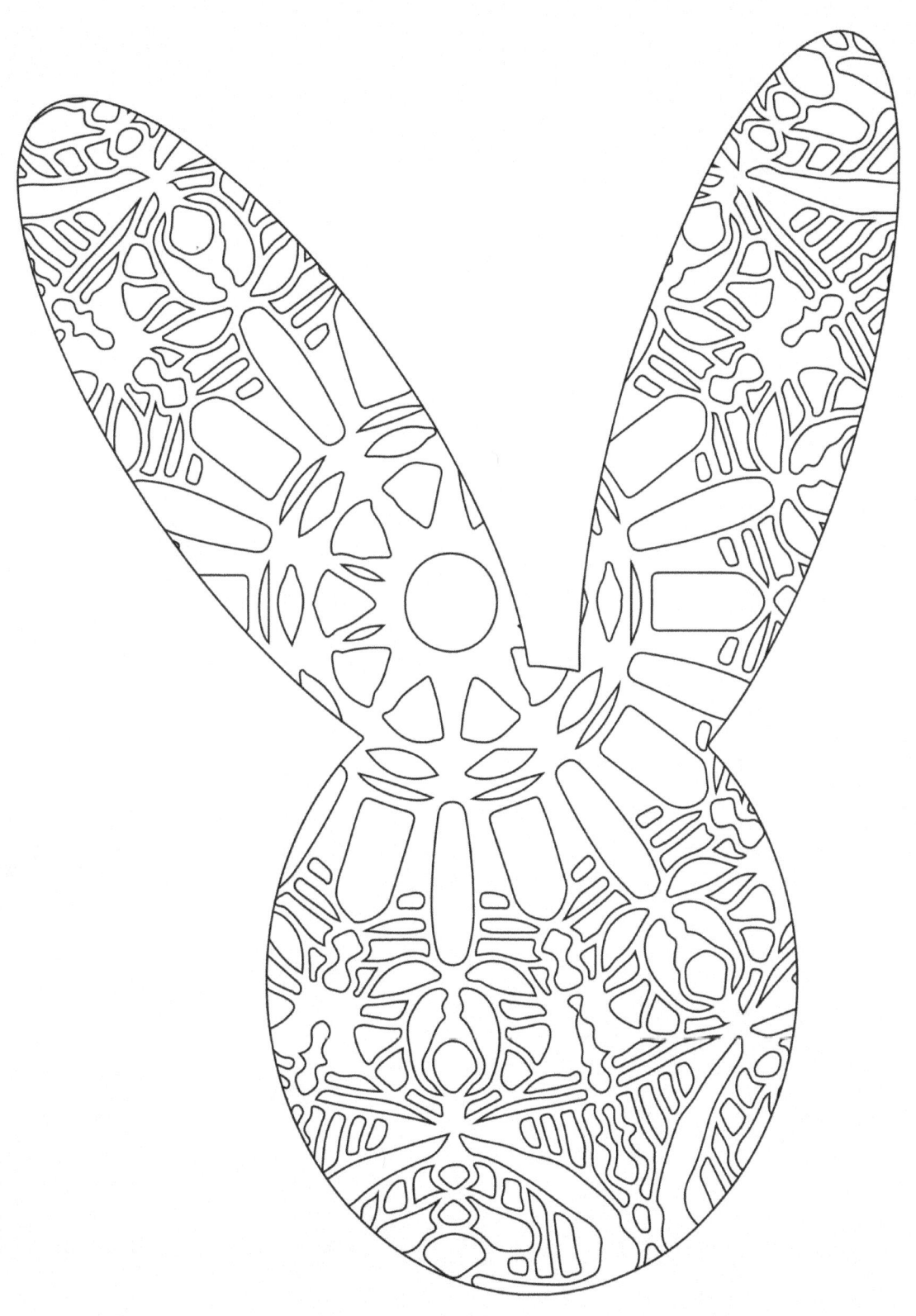

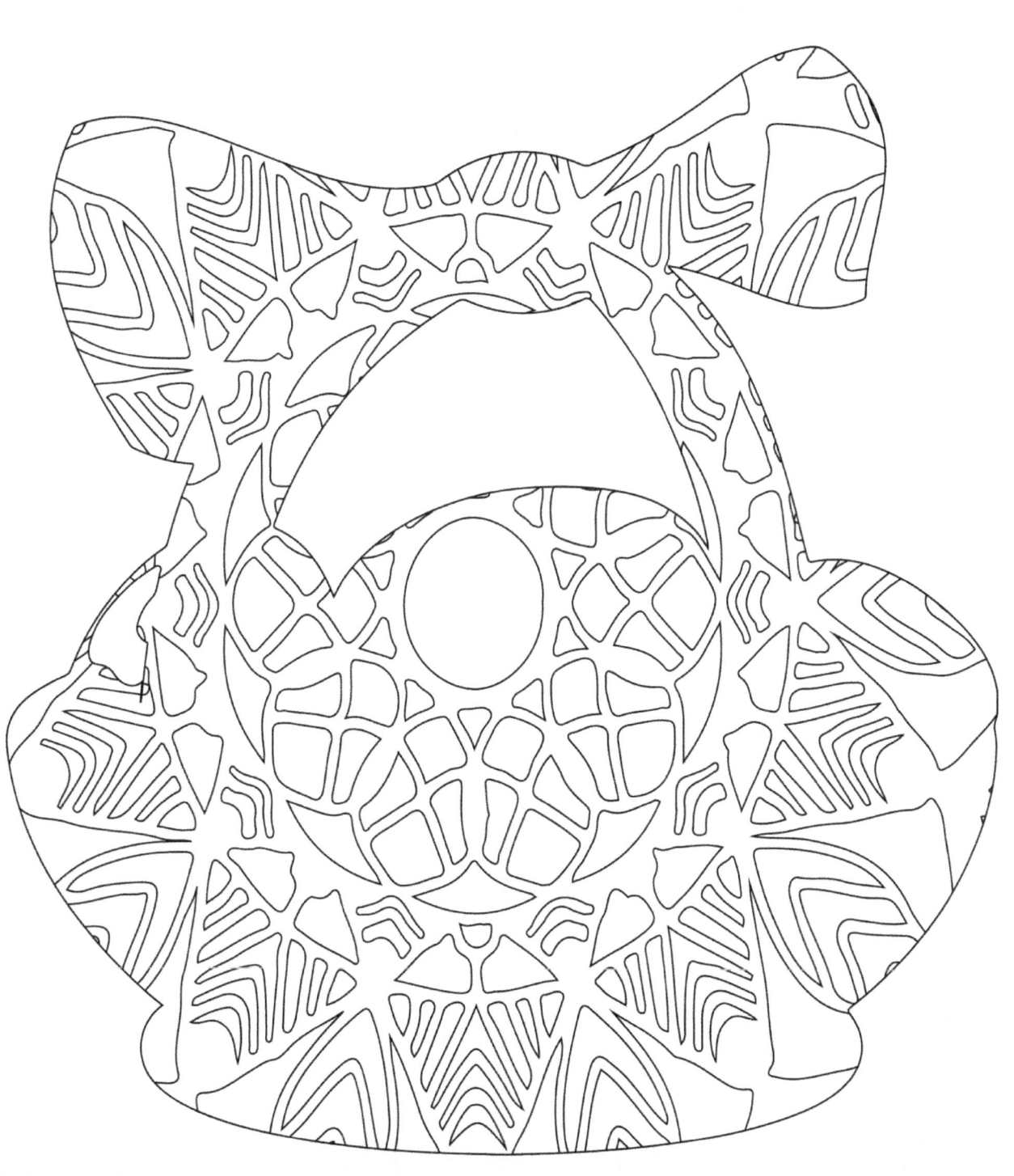

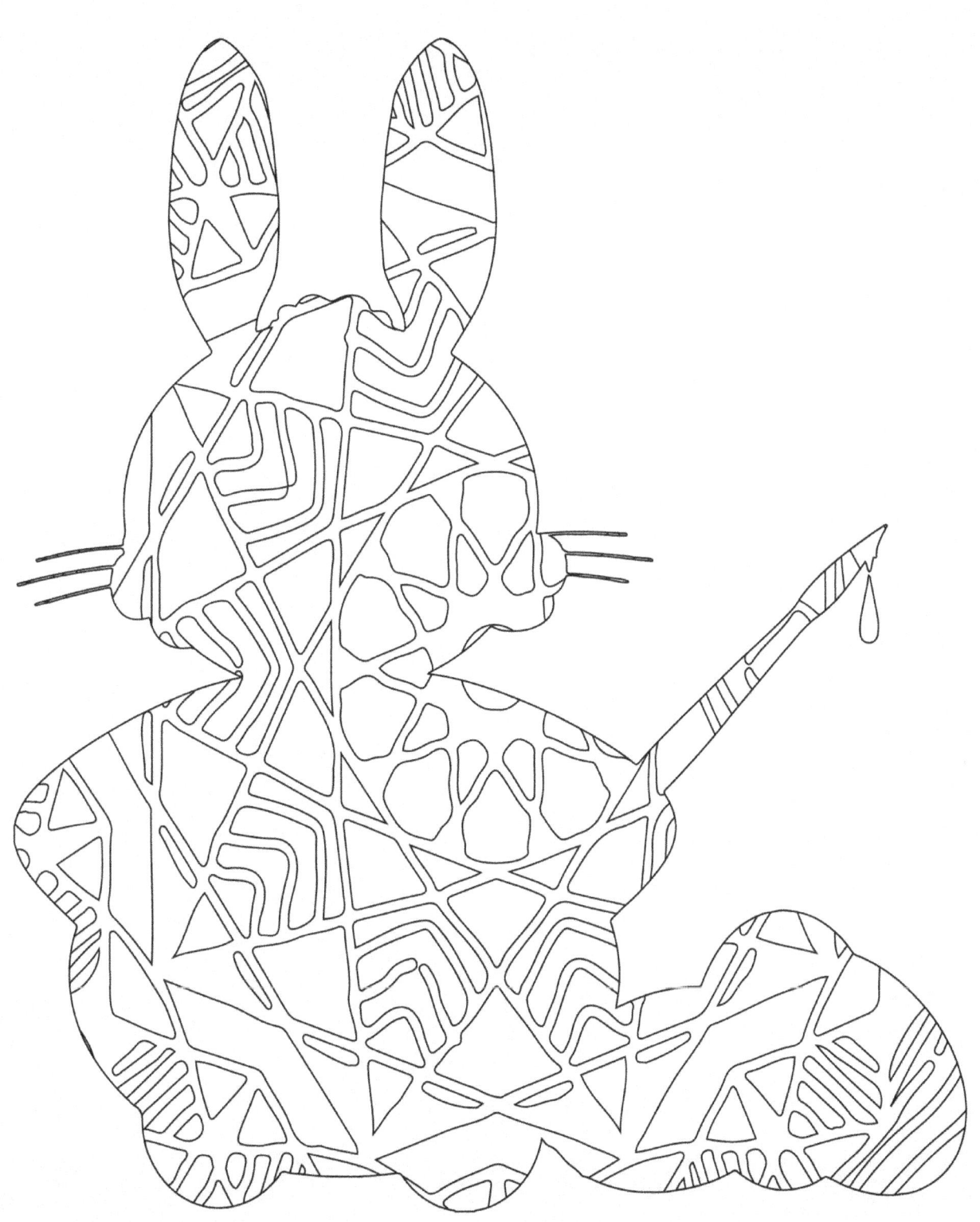

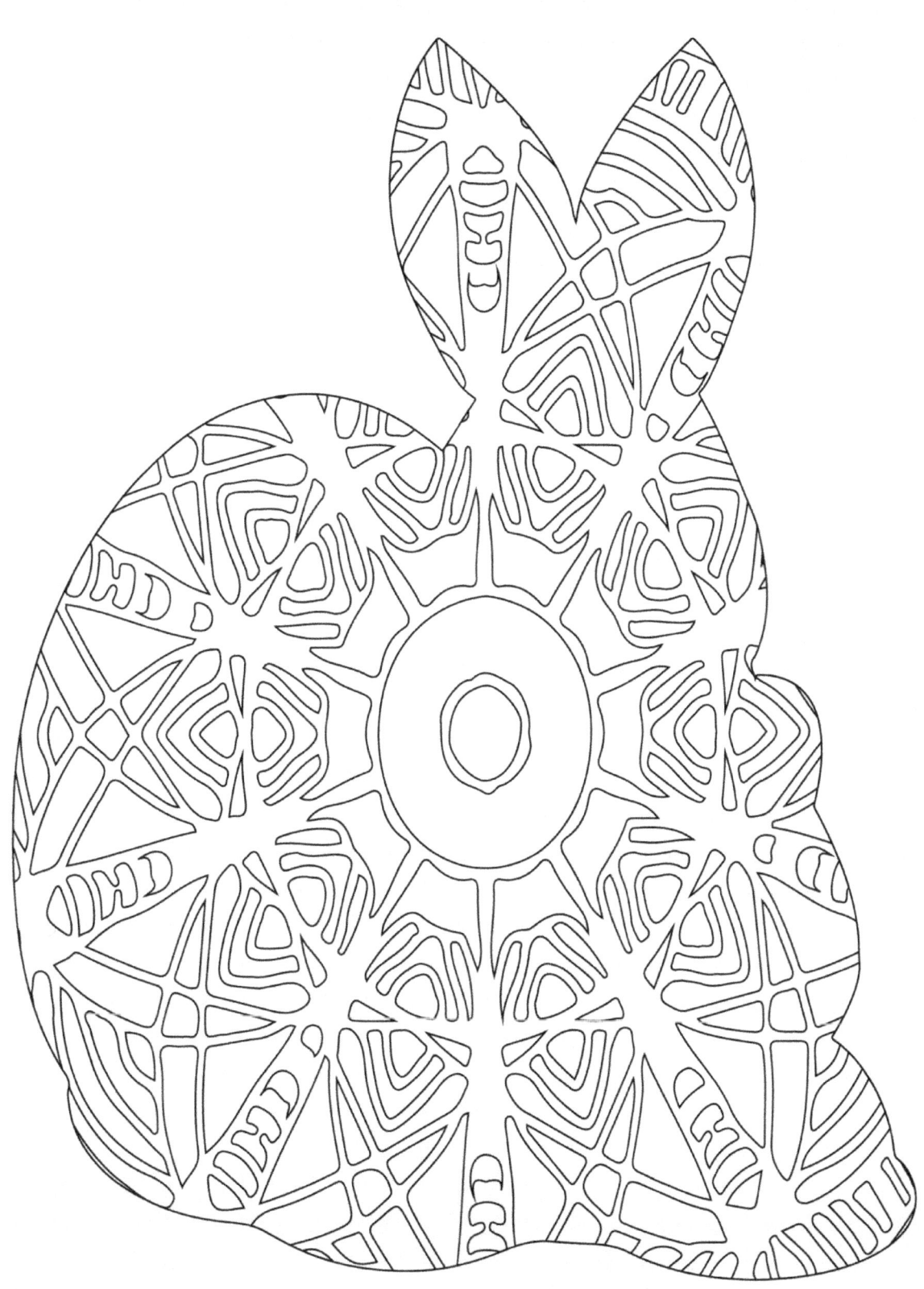

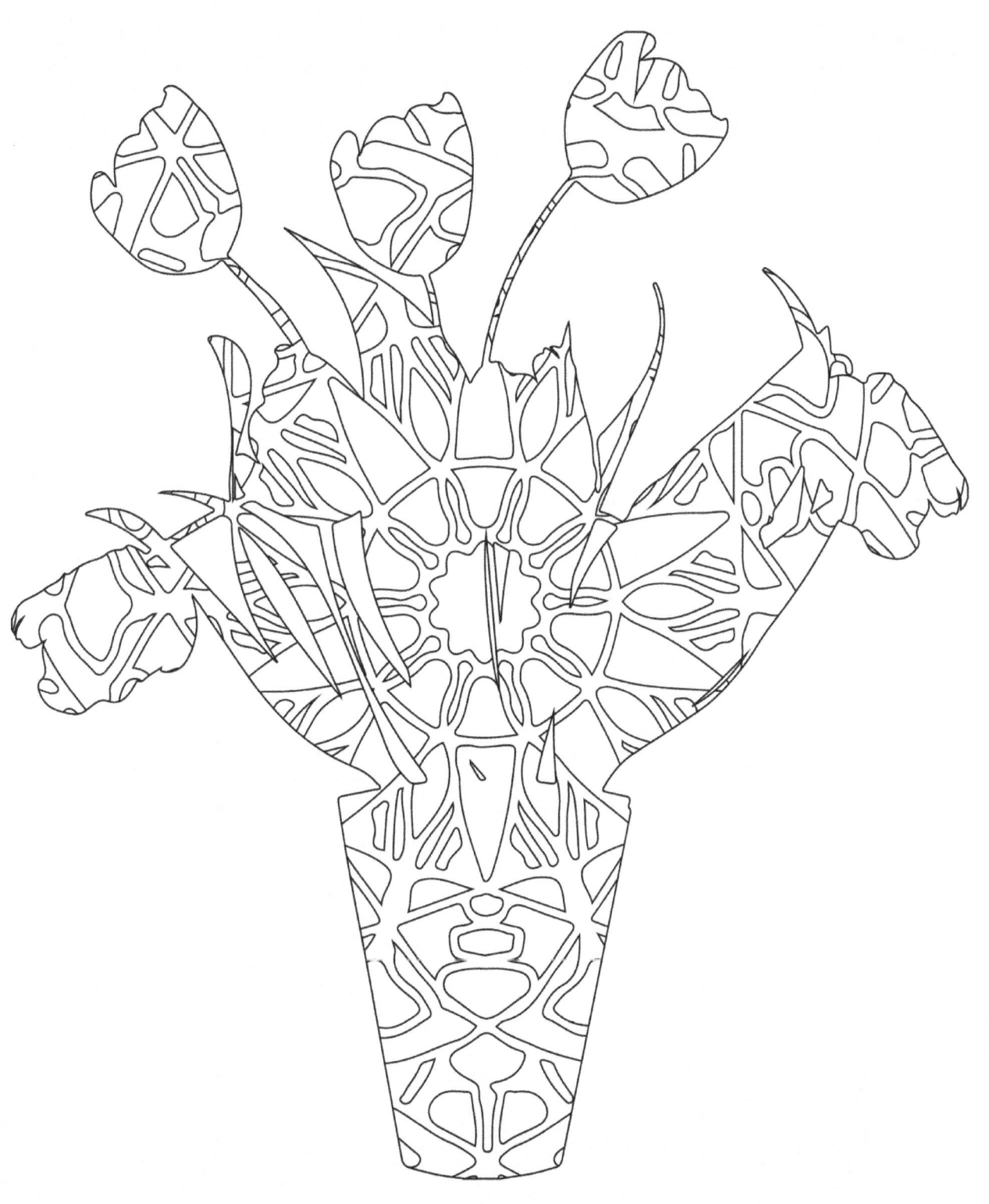

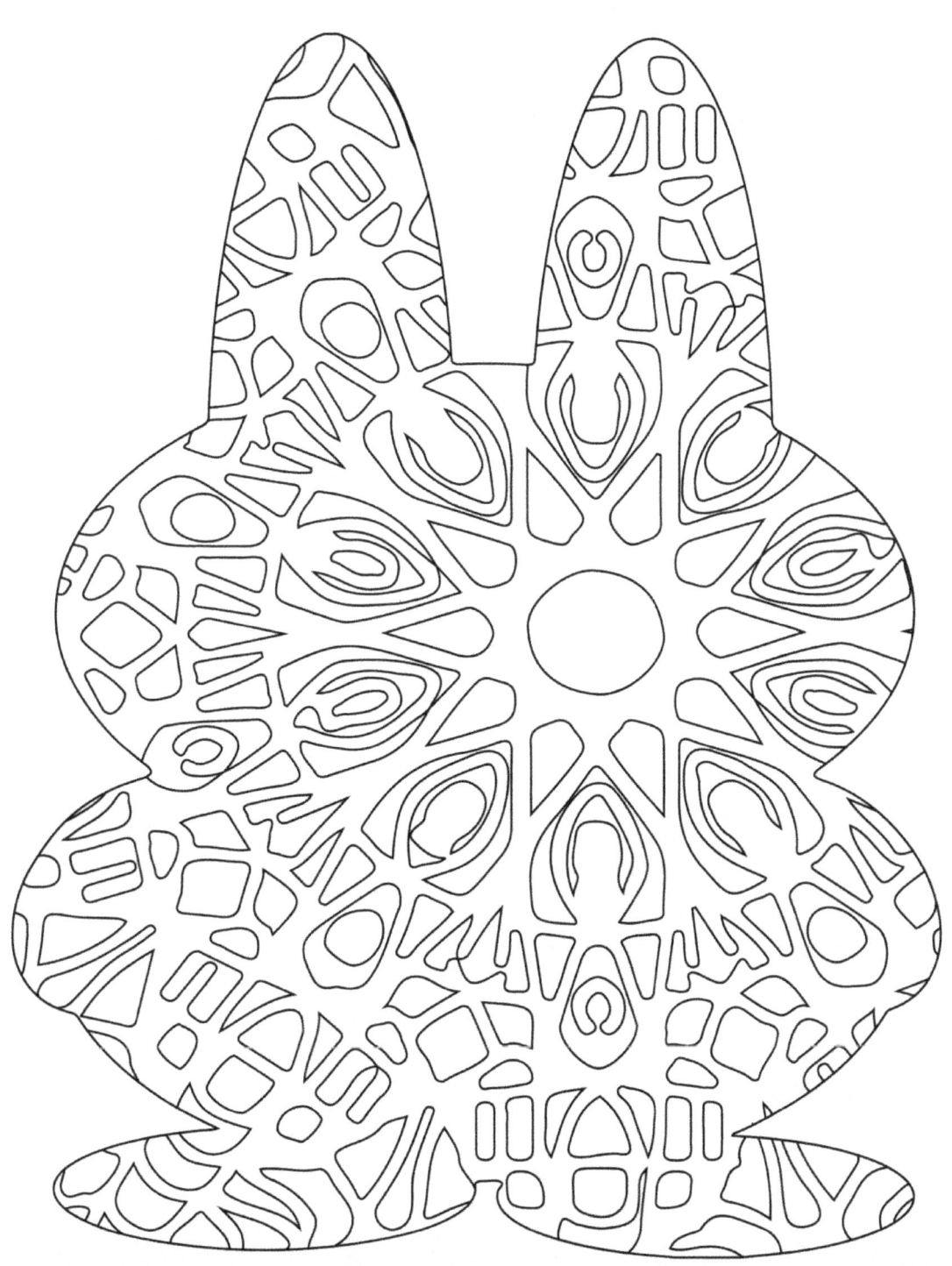

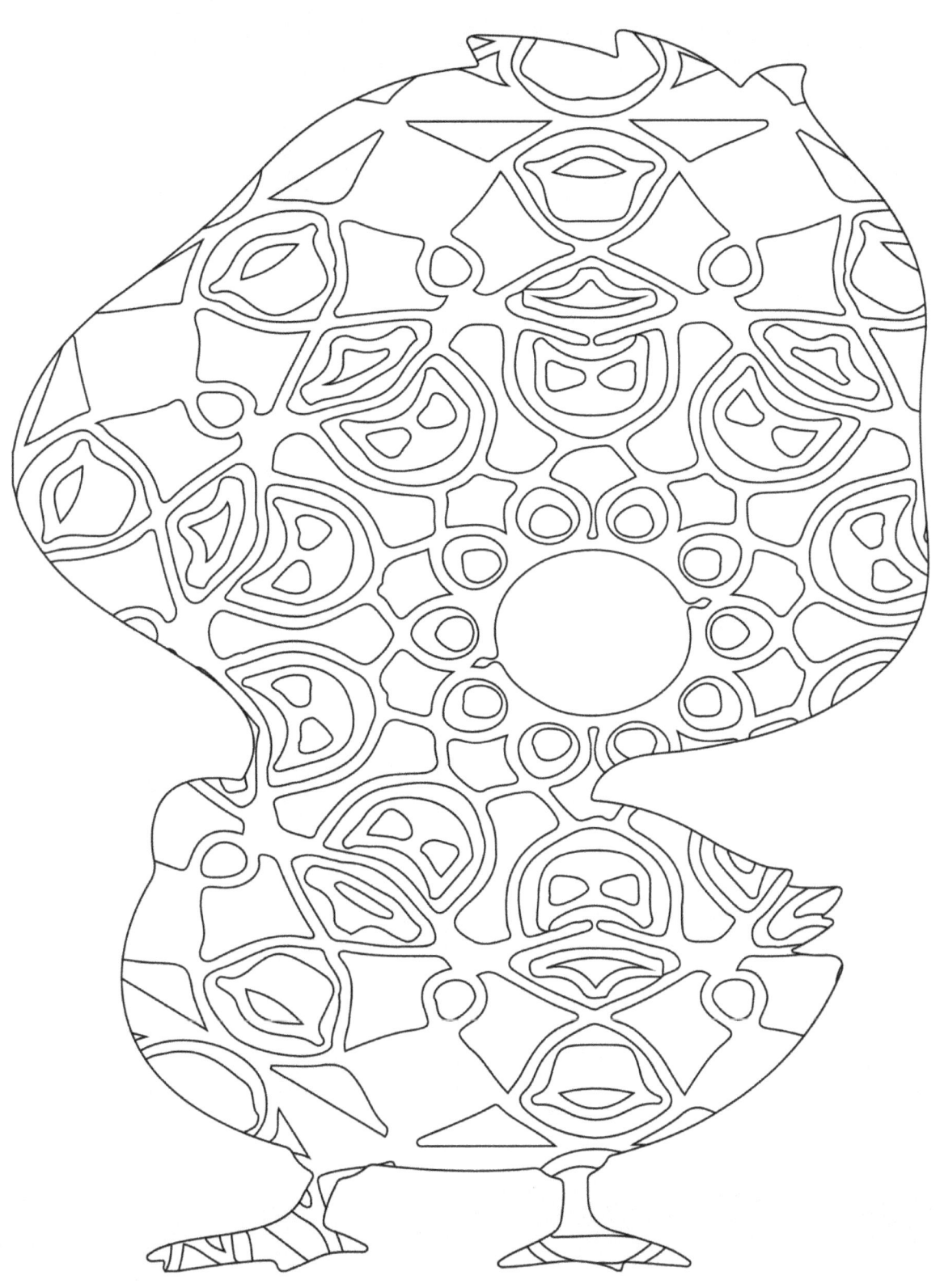

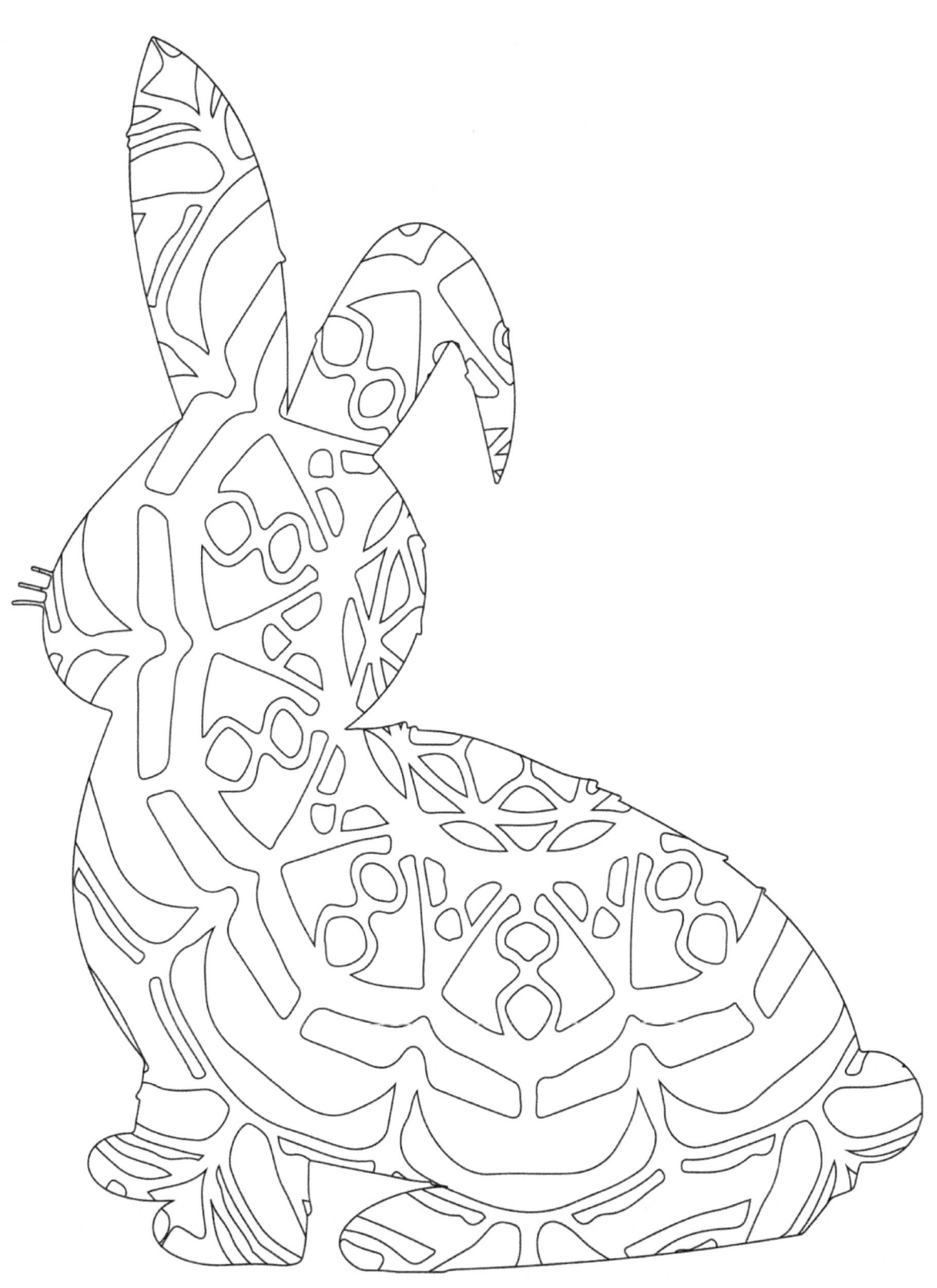

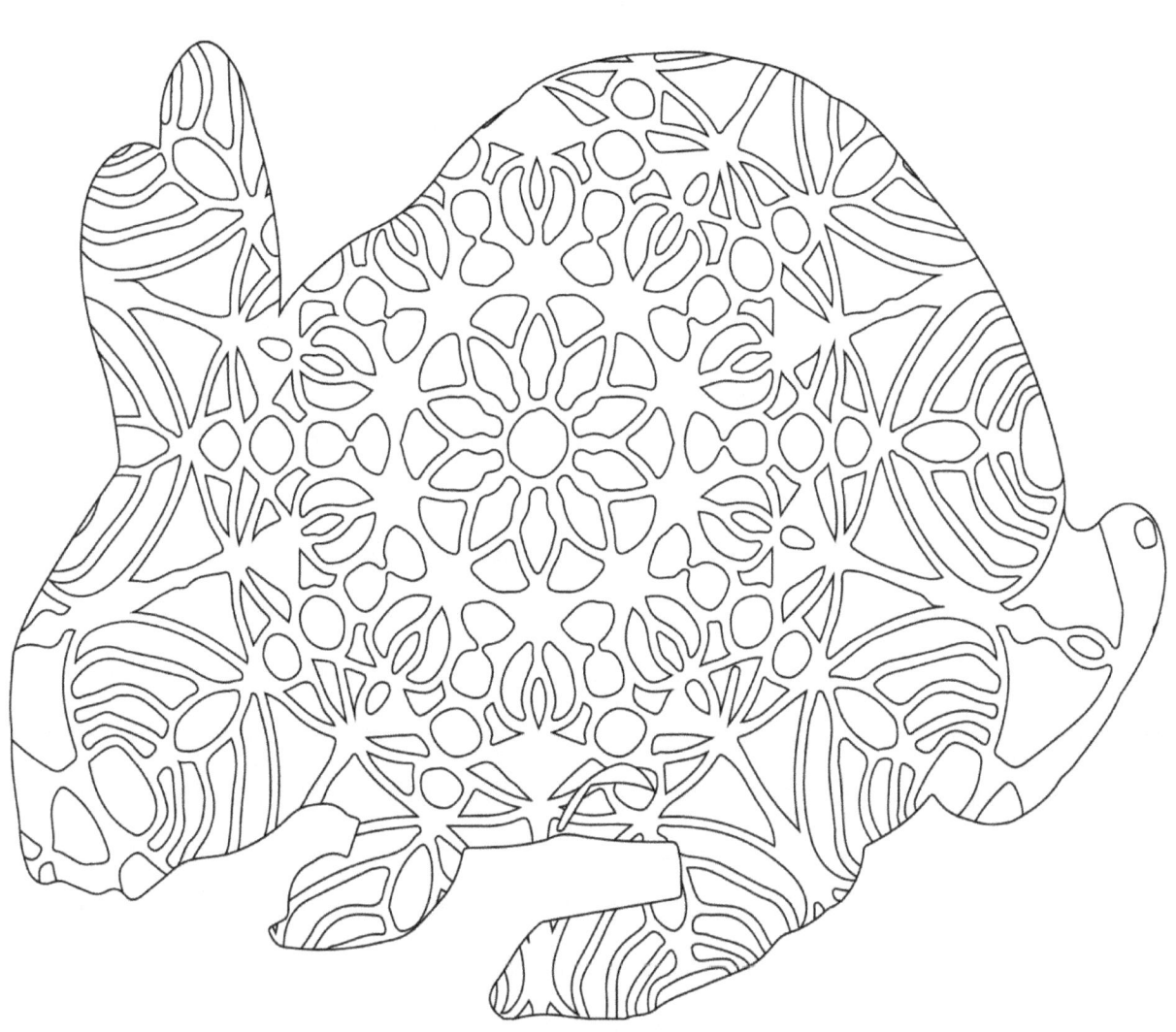

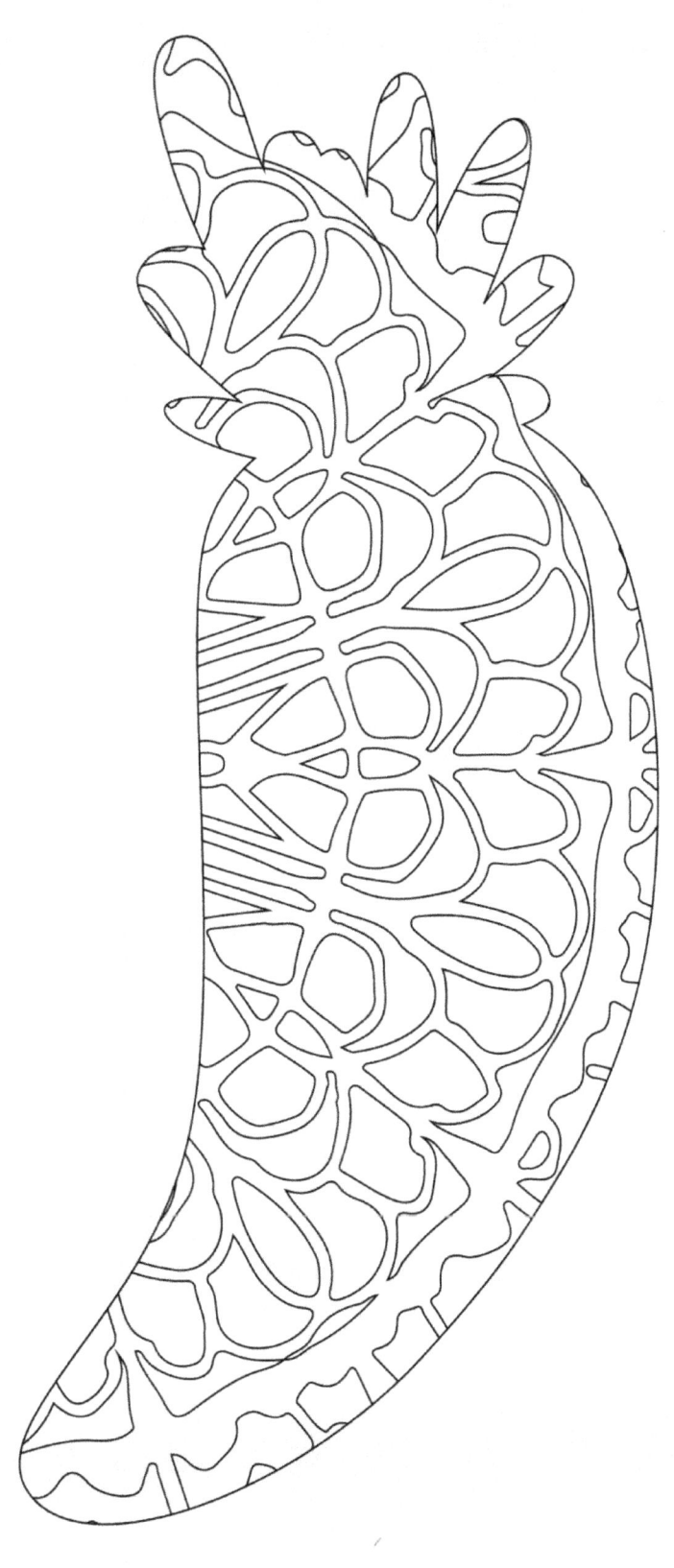

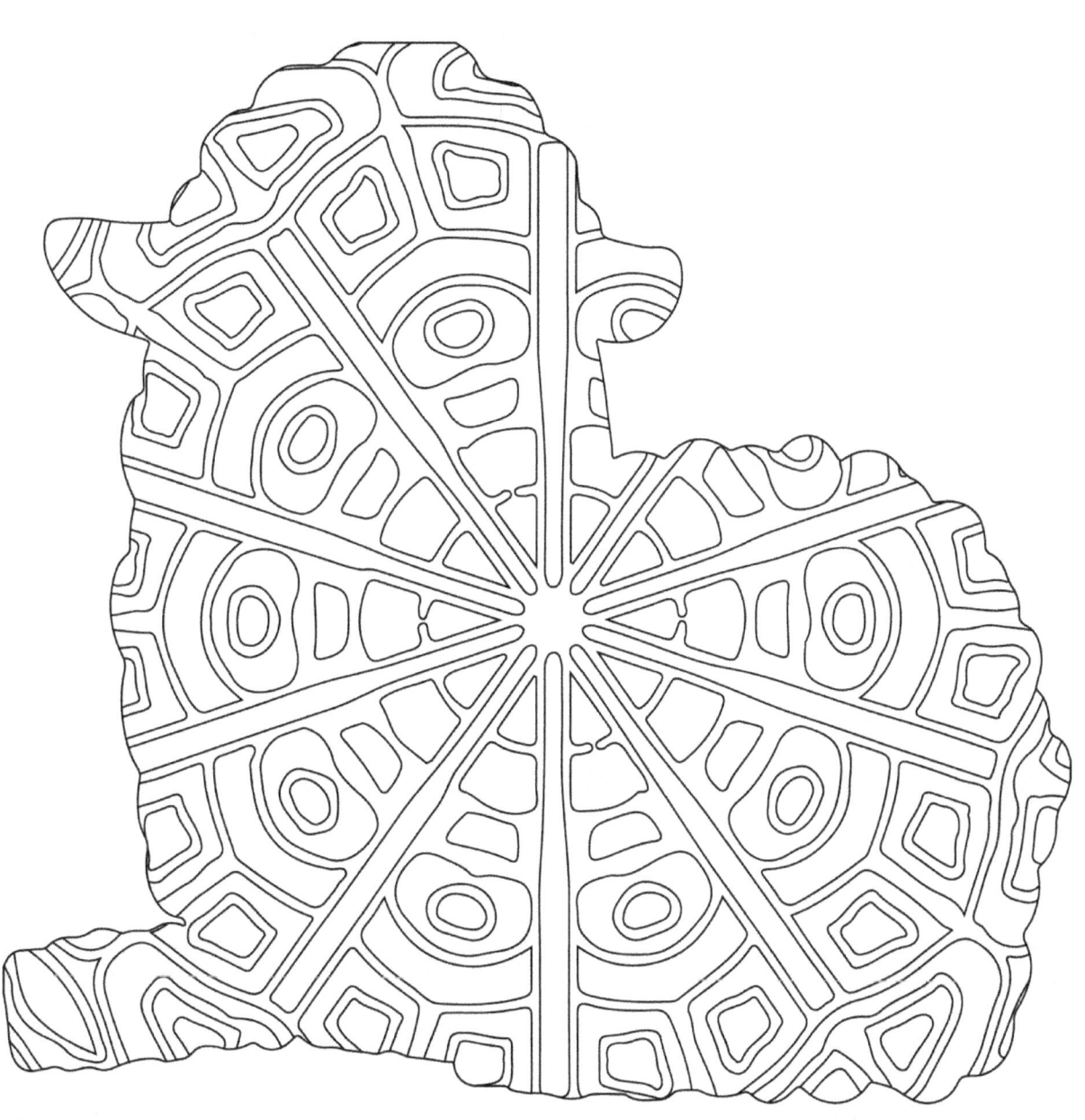

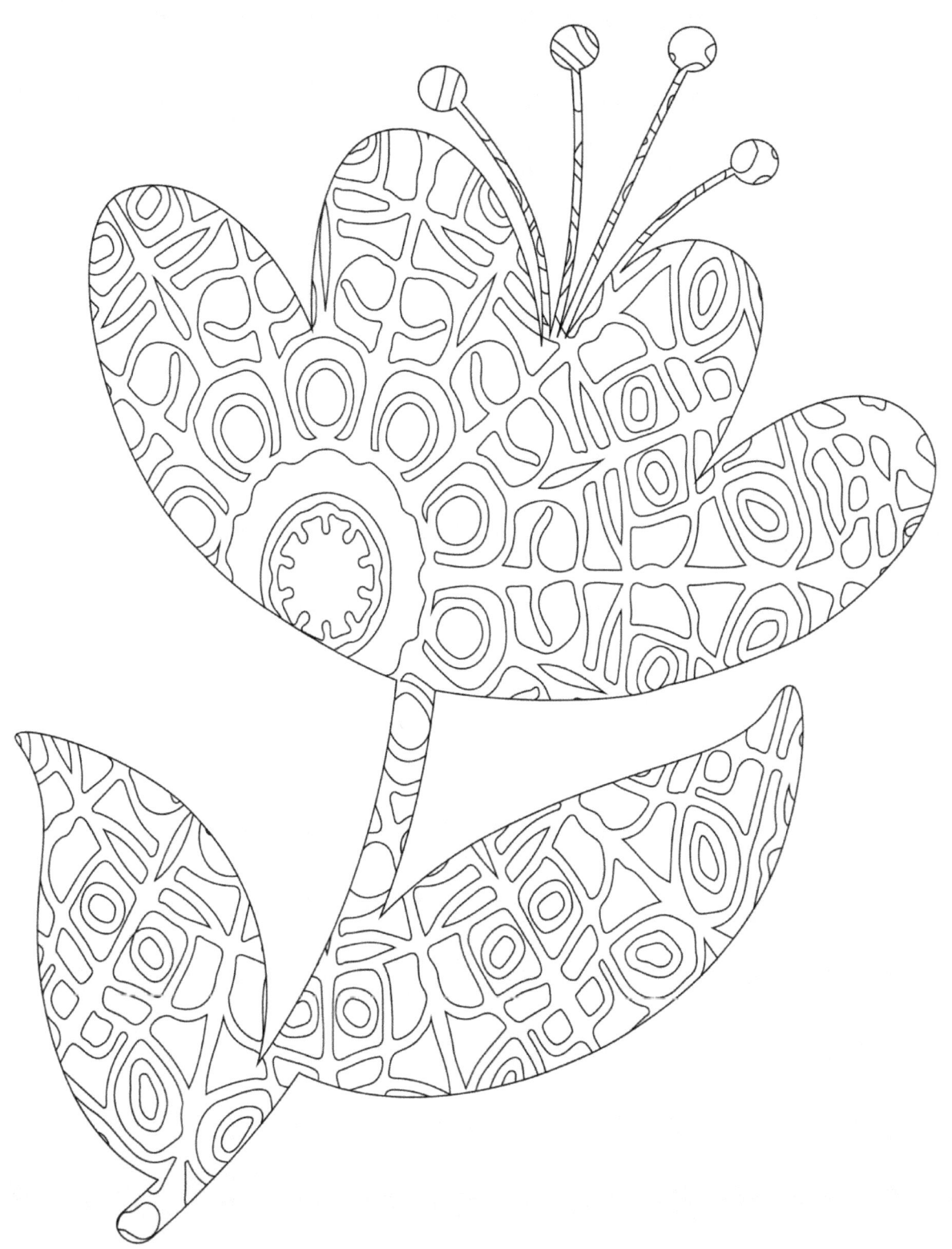

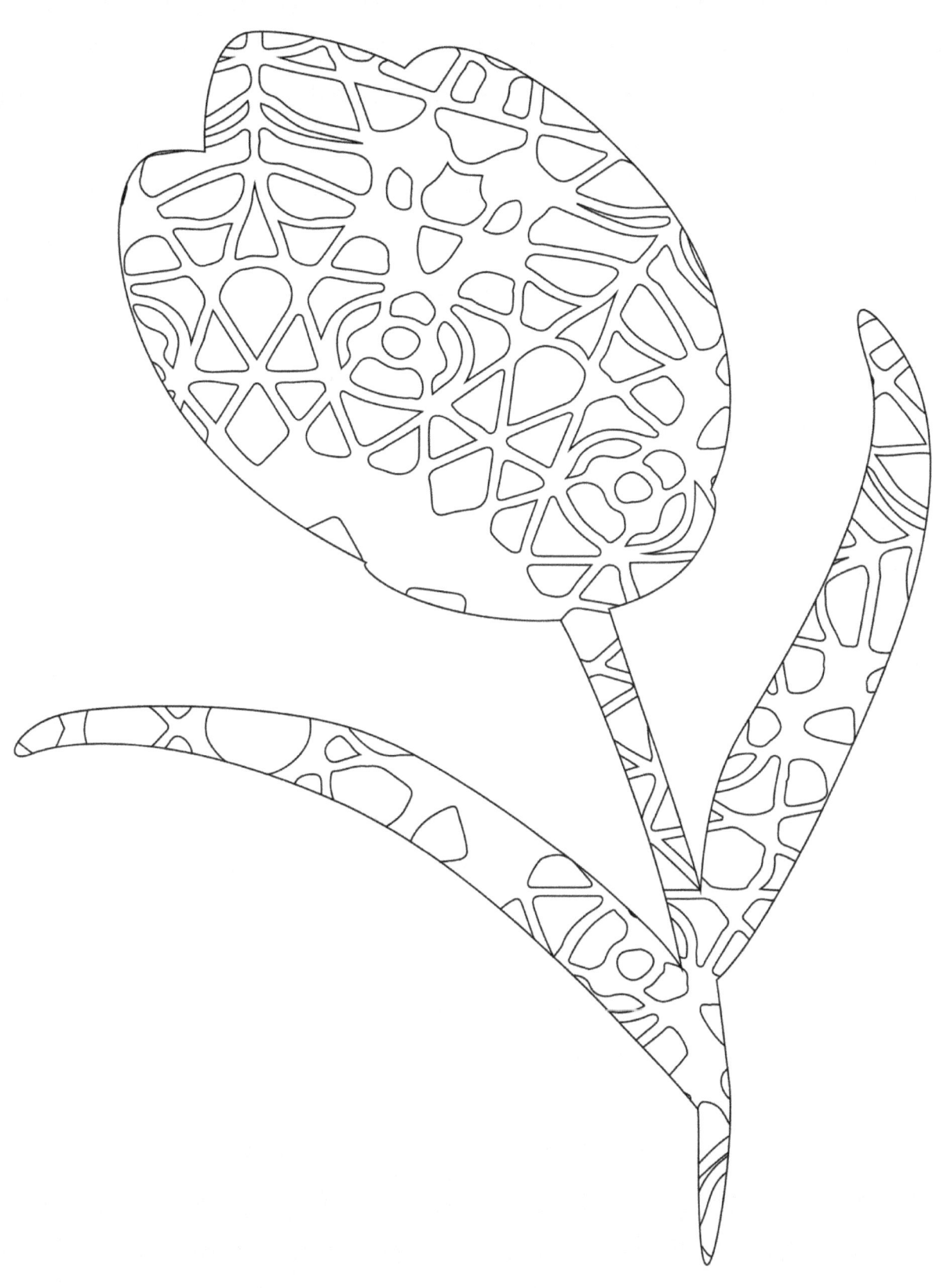

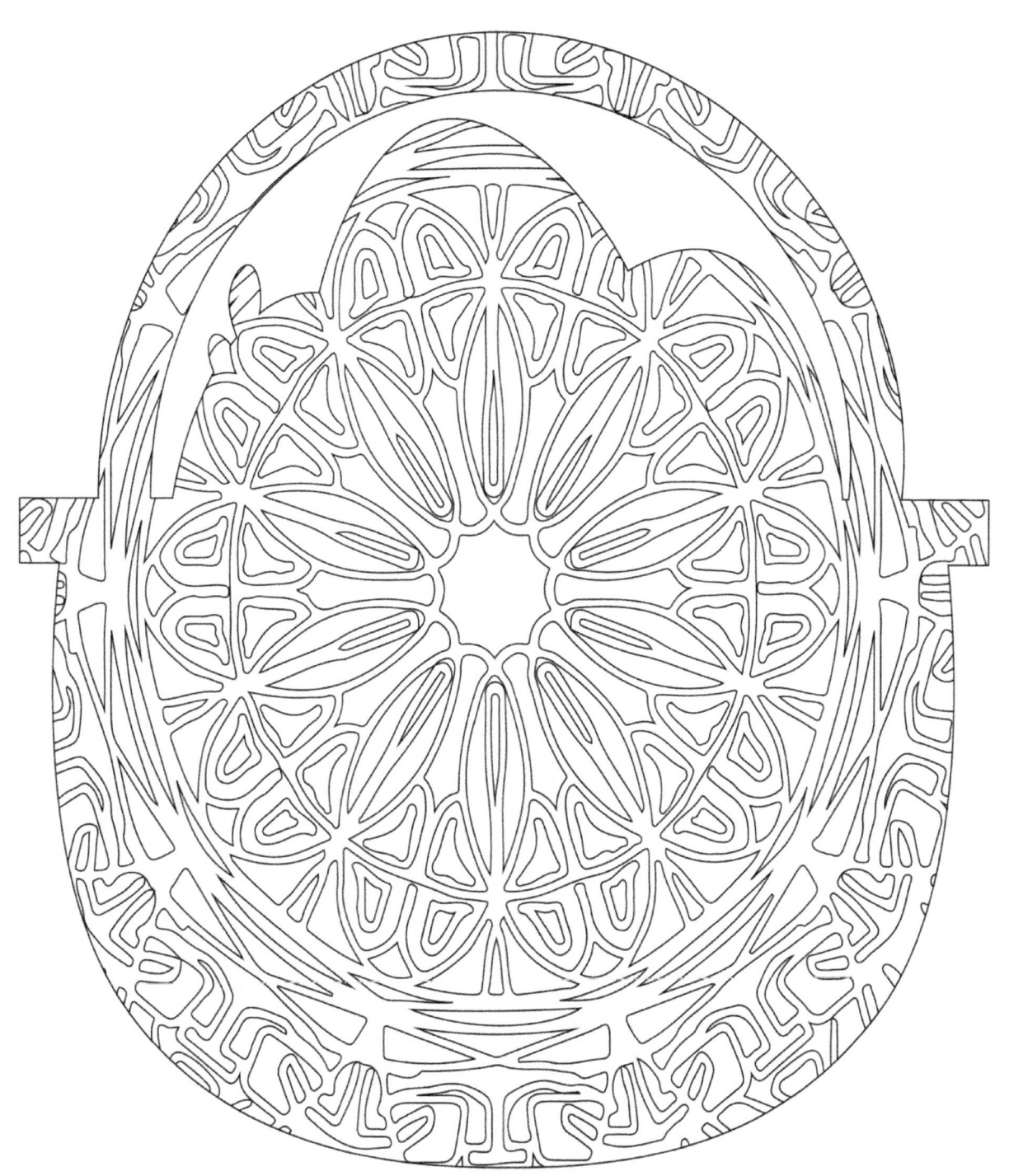

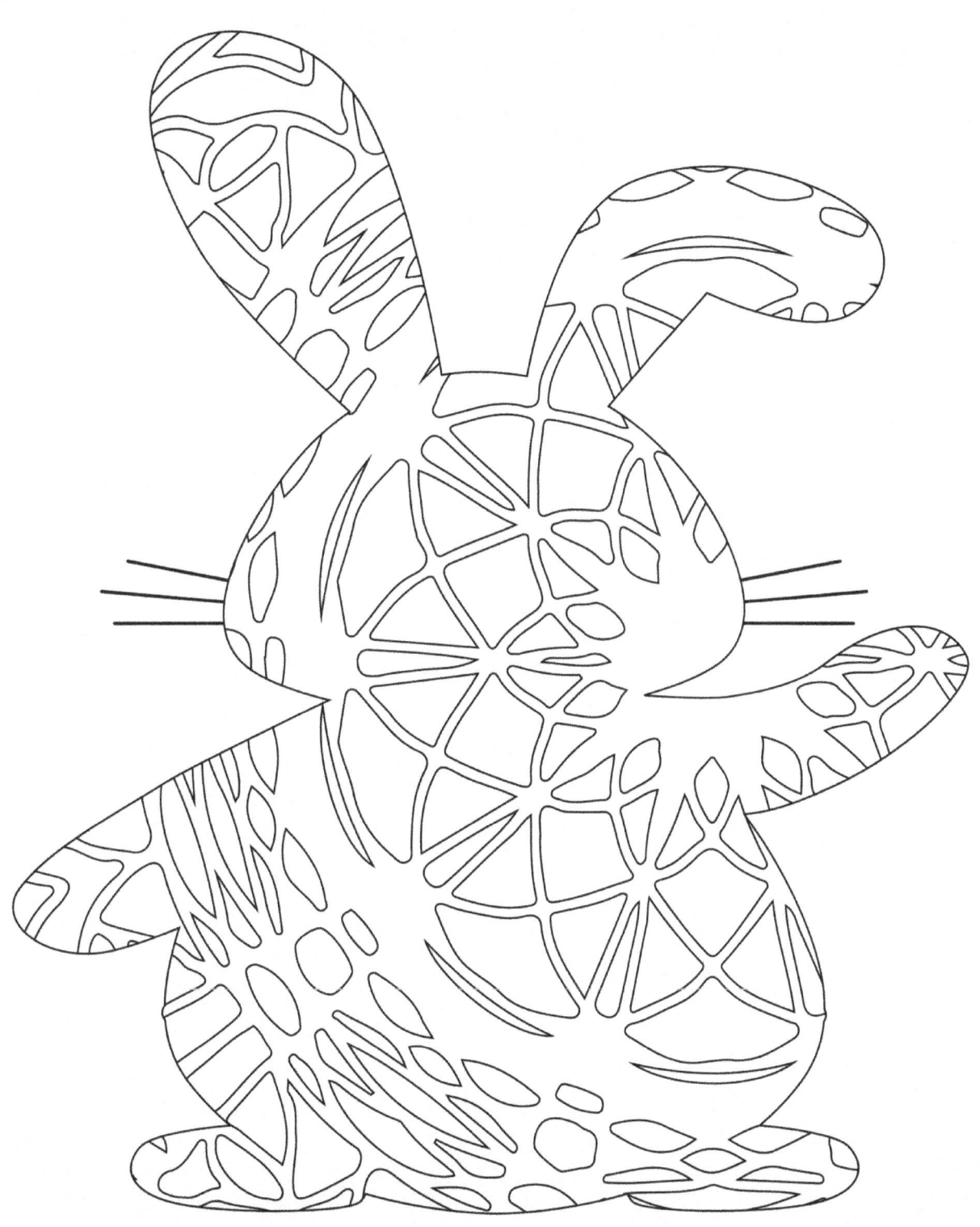

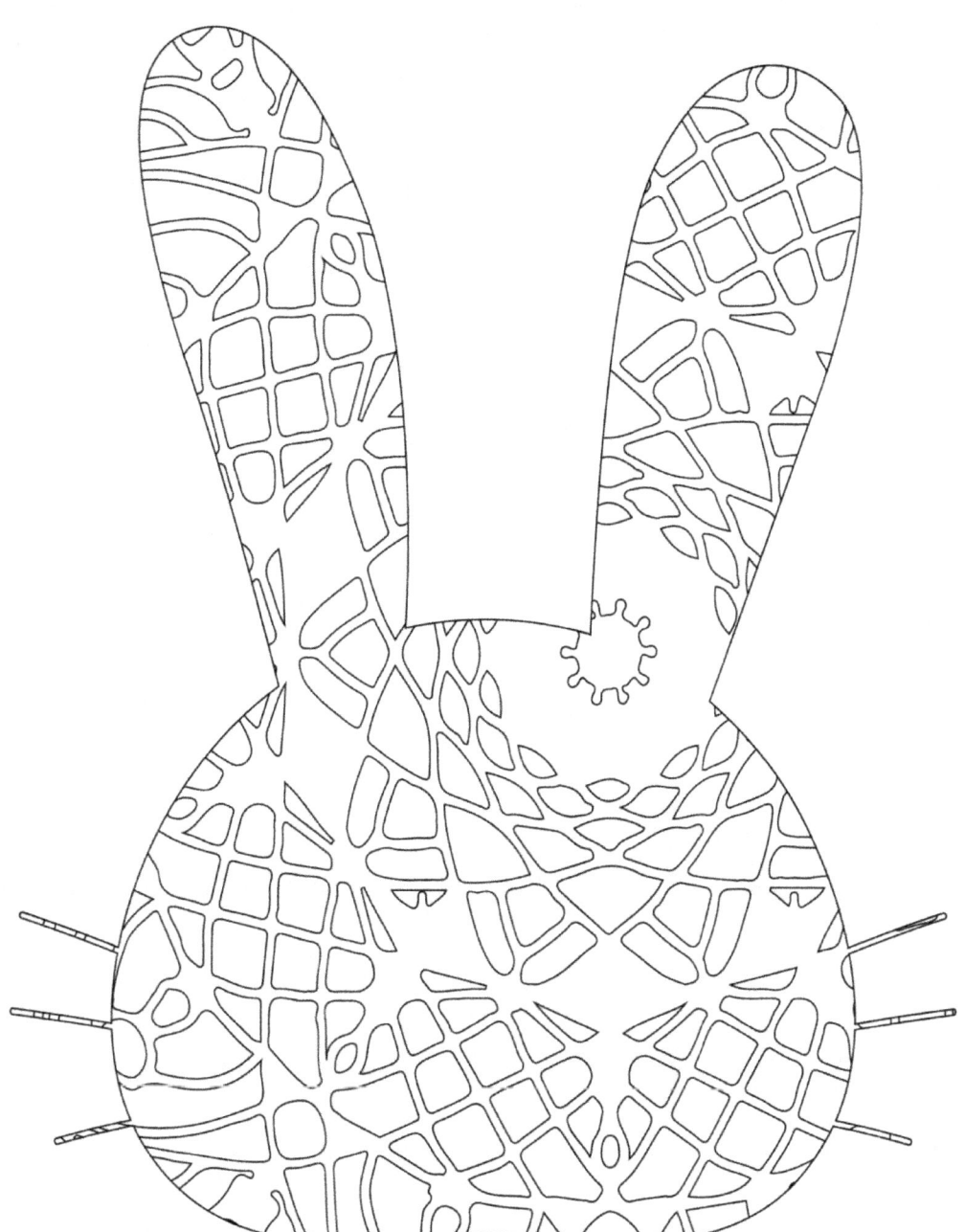

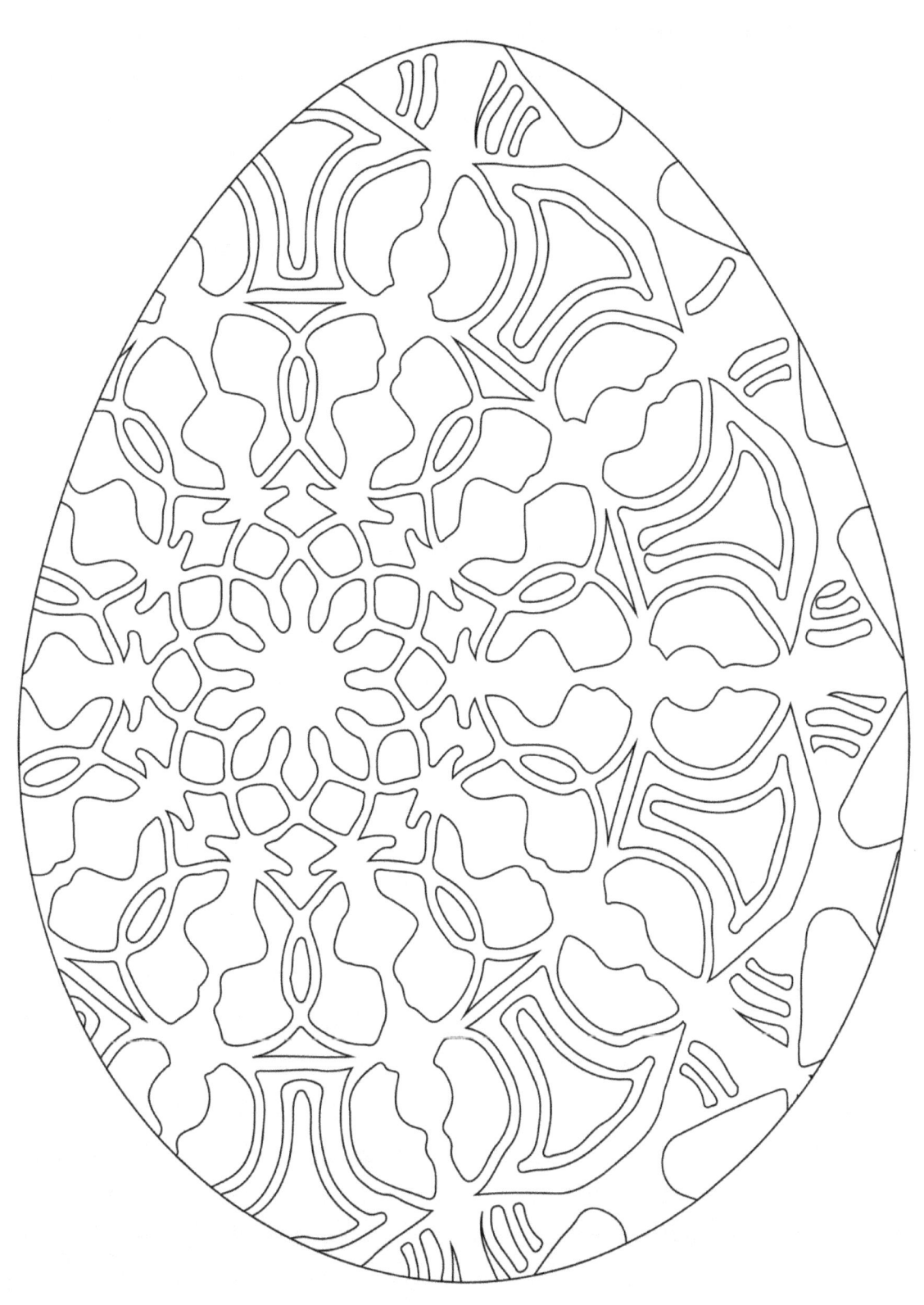

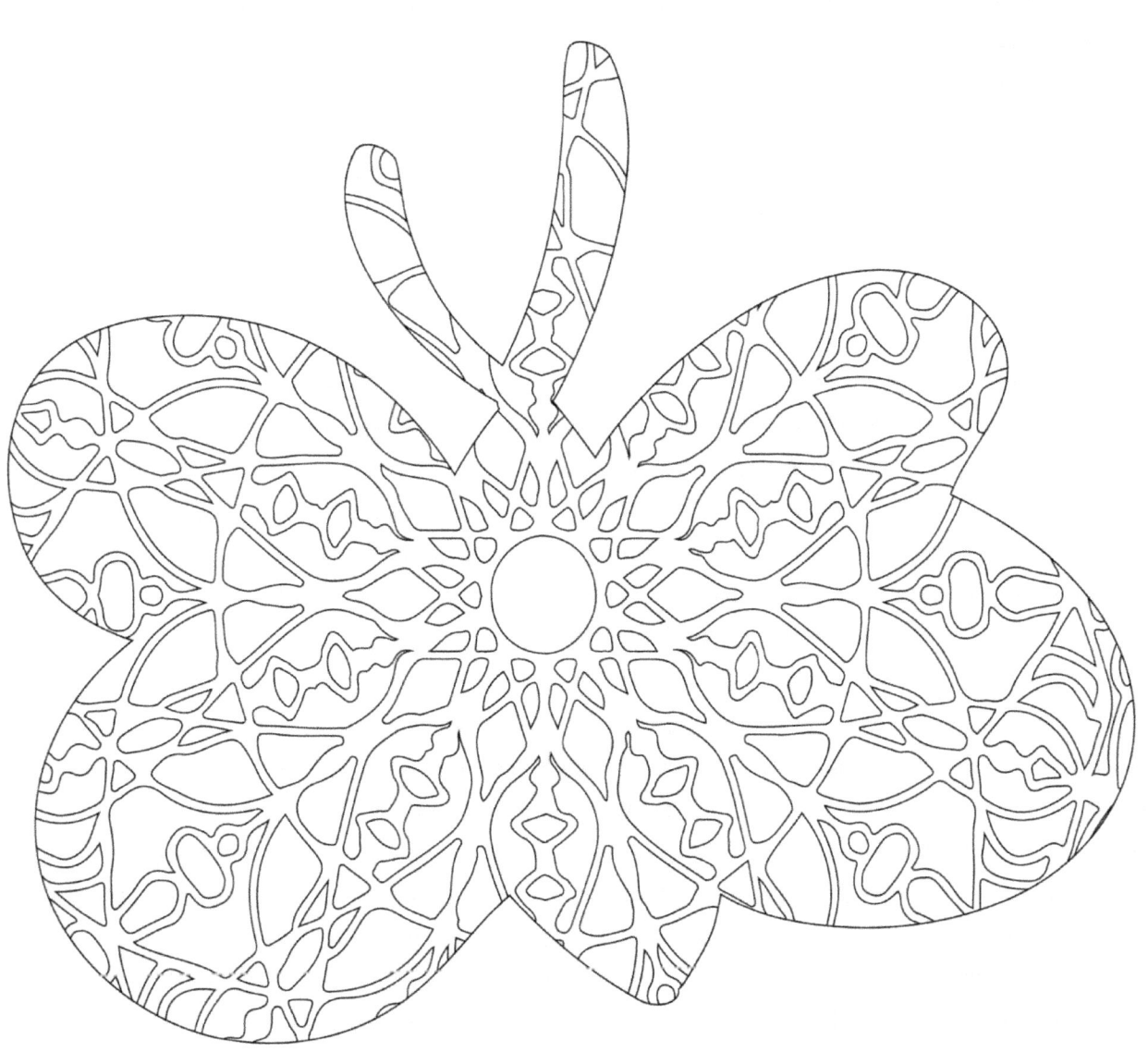

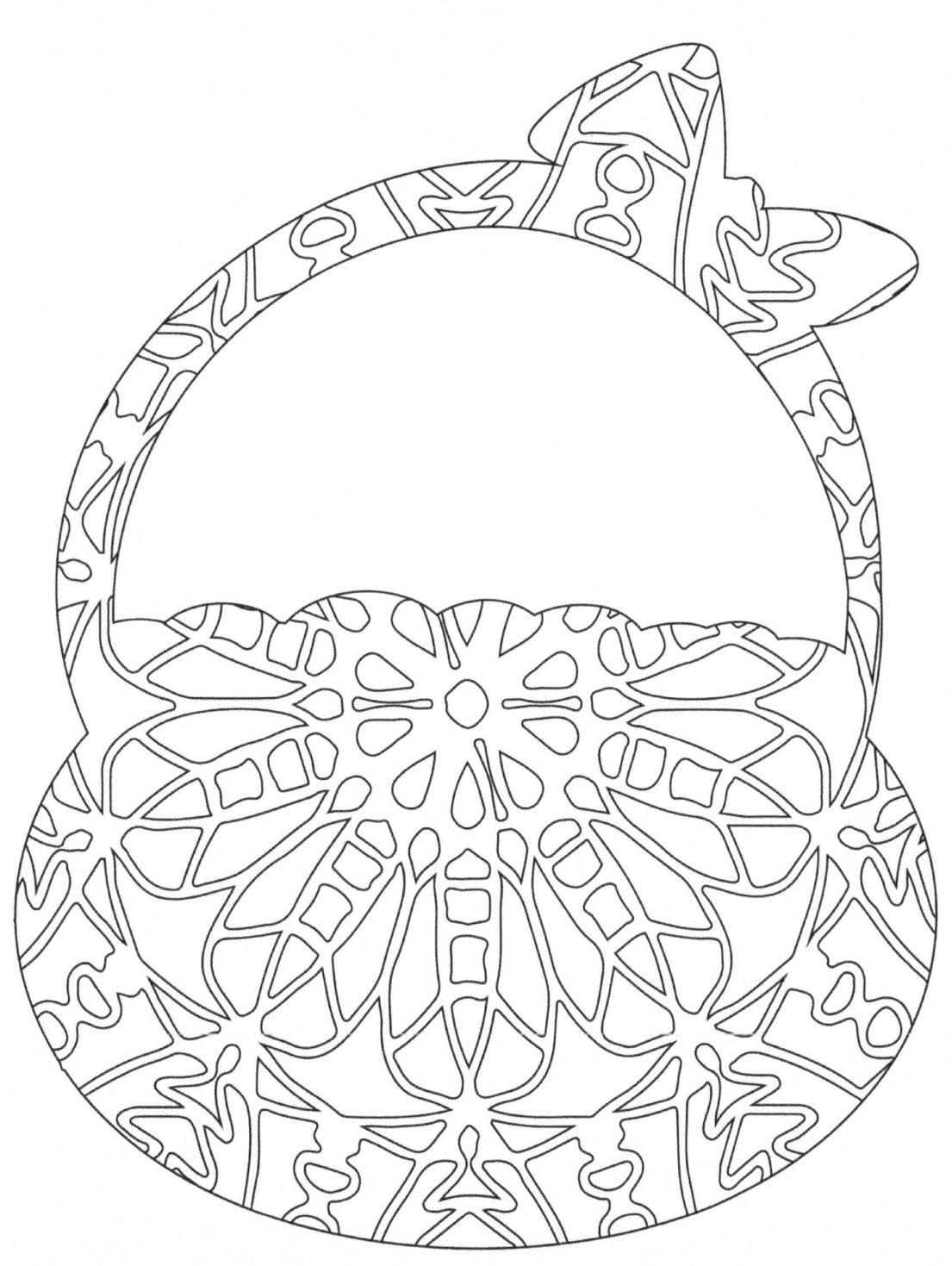

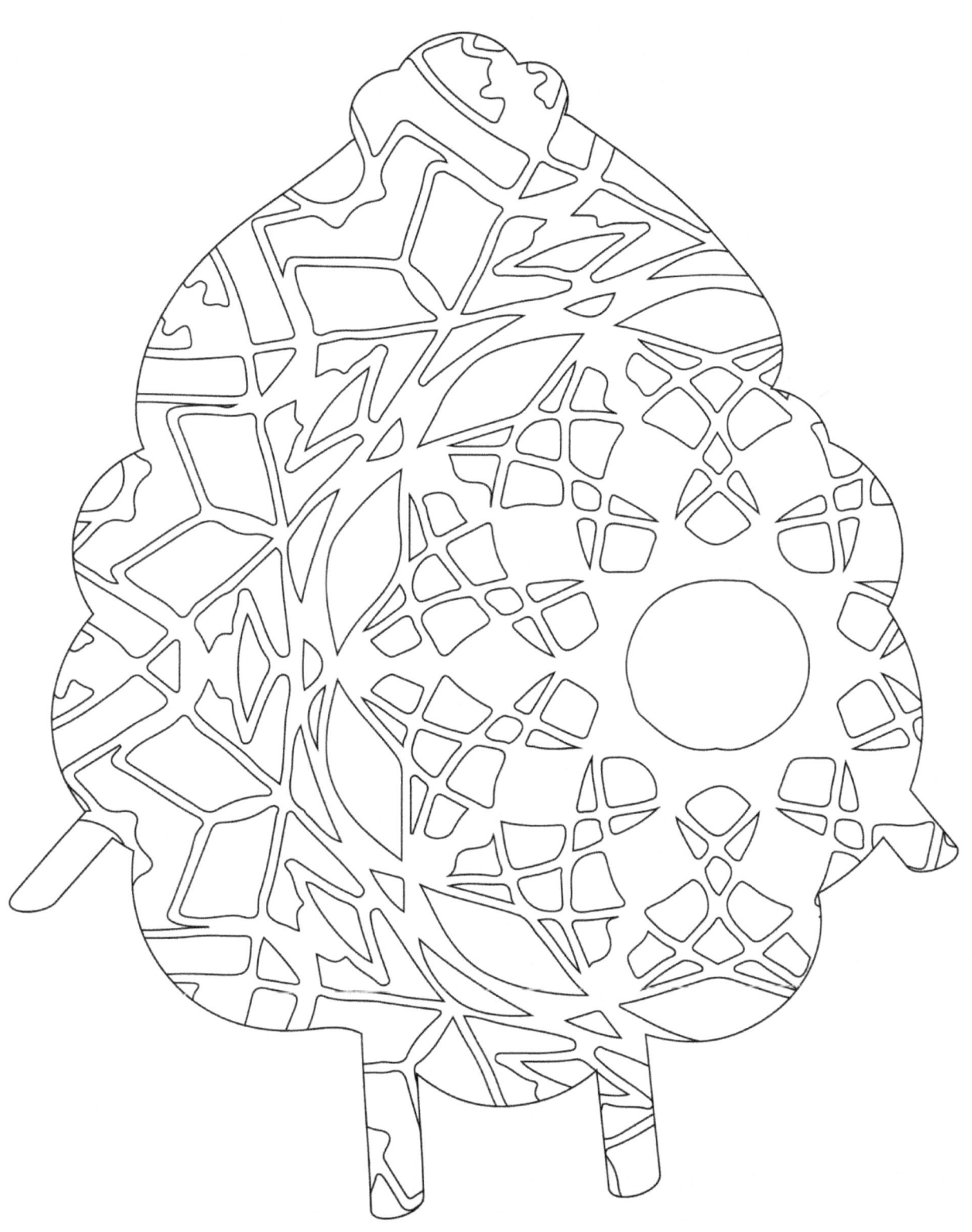

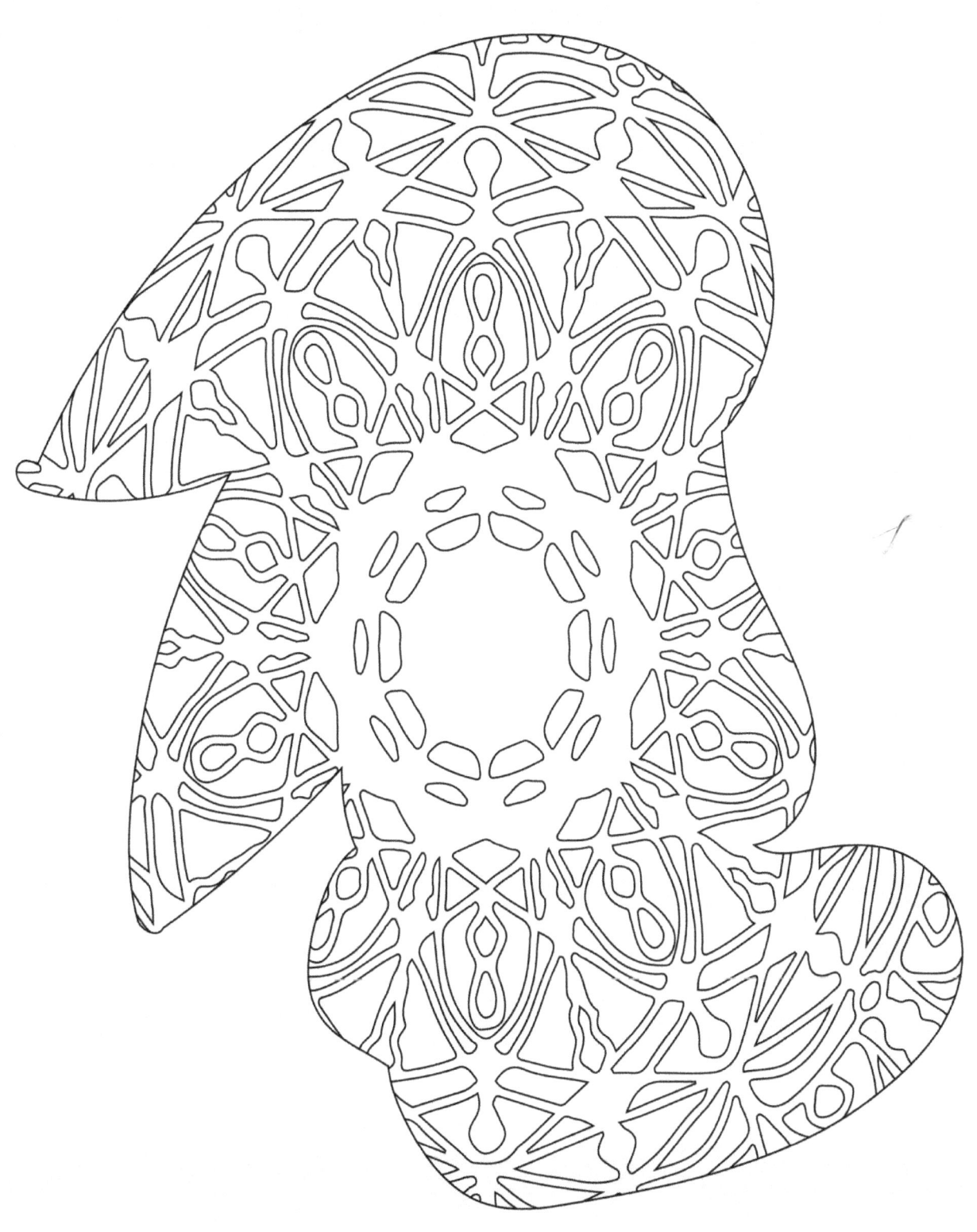

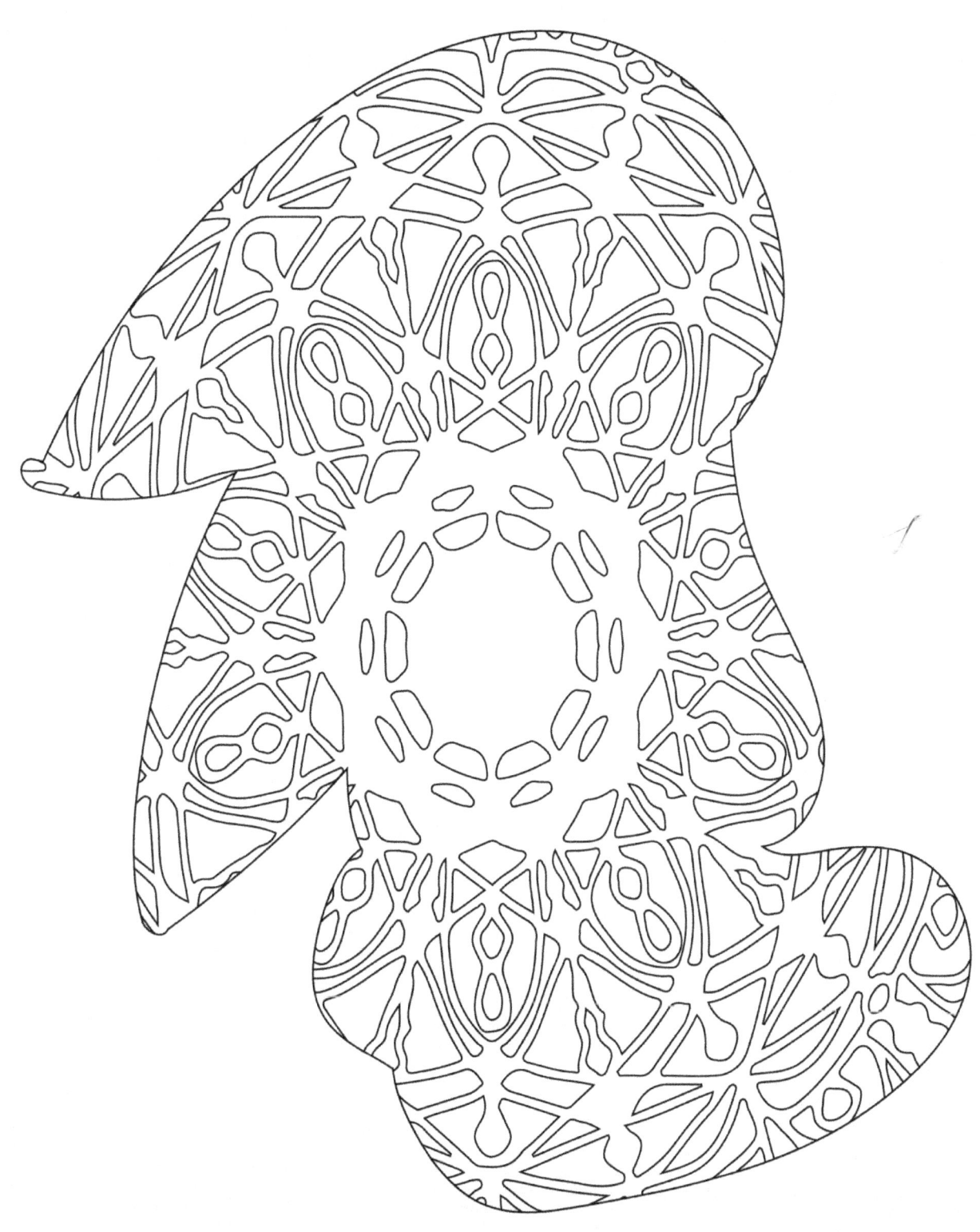

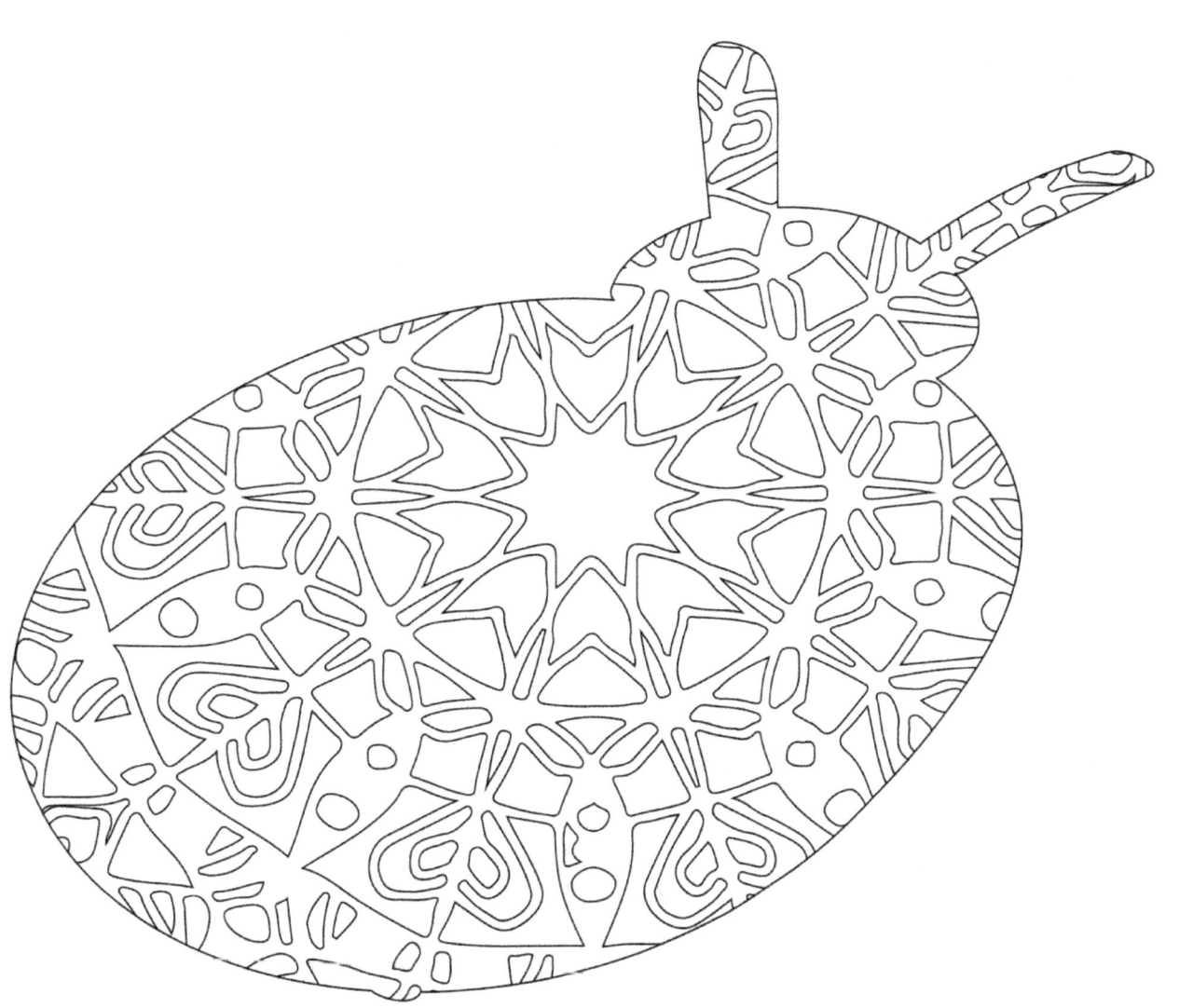

Thank you so much
for purchasing this Mandala coloring book,
if you enjoyed it, then please leave a
positive Amazon review.
Then we can help others to find out
about our books.

Cheers!

Joelma Lima